PORTRAIT
OF A
DECADE

Drought refugees, Abilene, Texas. Dorothea Lange.

LOUISIANA STATE UNIVERSITY PRESS
Baton Rouge

PORTRAIT OF A DECADE

Roy Stryker and the Development of Documentary Photography in the Thirties

F. JACK HURLEY

Photographic Editing by
ROBERT J. DOHERTY

For Katie Beth and Jim

ISBN 0-8071-0235-0

Library of Congress Catalog Card Number 72-79331

Copyright © 1972 by Louisiana State University Press

All rights reserved

Manufactured in the United States of America

Composition by University Graphics, Inc.,
Shrewsbury, New Jersey

Printing and binding by Halliday Lithograph Corp.,
West Hanover, Massachusetts

Designed by Albert R. Crochet

Quotation from *Land of the Free,*
copyright, 1938, 1966, by Archibald MacLeish,
reprinted by permission of
Harcourt Brace Jovanovich, Inc.

Unless otherwise indicated, all photographs included
herein were taken from the Roy Stryker Collection and
are reproduced with the permission of the University
of Louisville Photographic Archive, Louisville, Kentucky.
Original negatives and prints of all photographs are in the
FSA and OWI files, Prints and Photographs Division,
Library of Congress.

Acknowledgments

Many people helped make this book possible. Bennett H. Wall at Tulane University first saw the possibilities contained in the idea, and he worked with great patience to sharpen and clarify my thoughts. The late William R. Hogan spent a great deal of time on the technical aspects of the book. Robert J. Doherty and Donald R. Anderson, at the University of Louisville, time after time, gave aid in crisis. In addition, Bob Doherty rendered yeoman service in selecting the photographs. His fine taste pervades the book.

Garnett McCoy, at the Archives of American Art in Detroit, opened to me the wonderful collection of interviews that Richard K. Doud conducted with nearly everyone who played a role in the FSA documentary project. Those interviews, with their rich insights, were a revelation to me. Memphis State University provided the all-important ingredient, money, and the excellent facilities of its Office of Oral History Research. The entire staff of the Prints and Photographs Division of the Library of Congress gave me their enthusiastic support. The list could go on and on for my debts are many and real.

Finally, it should be noted that this book was enriched by the cooperation I received from many people who were involved in the FSA documentary project. When busy people take time to discuss events that happened years ago with a young graduate student whom they hardly know, it bespeaks a love of the subject and a humanity that are unusual. Russell Lee, Arthur Rothstein, and, most of all, Roy Stryker, this book is for you.

Introduction

Serious still photography, like the more conventional forms of
art, has long been rent by a division. There are those who insist
that the proper use of the camera is to explore the inner reaches
of man's mind, his ideas and his ideals. Often this approach has
led to pictorial romanticism and a tendency to regard the photograph as an end in itself. Others have preferred to turn the camera
outward and use it as a means of understanding man and his
environment. This style, too, has its dangers. It may degenerate
into a plea for pity; it may become so committed to a search for
"relevance" that it becomes a sermon rather than a photograph.
In the hands of a mature artist, however, the documentary style
of photography may laugh or cry, or do both. It may teach; it may
provoke a negative reaction. But whatever else, a good documentary photograph is never neutral. It has a point of view.

No one person or group of persons invented the modern documentary photograph. The tradition of using photographs to show
reality with a point of view dates back to the beginning of photography. In the United States, Mathew Brady was certainly within
the documentary tradition when he dispatched his photographers
to the battlefields of the Civil War. Jacob Riis's work in the slums
of New York around 1890 and Lewis Hine's pictures of the evils
of child labor for the magazine *Charities and Commons* prior
to World War I were facets of the documentary tradition. On a
subtler level, Paul Strand's pictures of Mexico and his beautiful
work in American towns were documents of the highest order.

Having said this, however, it must be acknowledged that there
was a turning point in the history of this esthetic style when it
became far more important than it had been before. That point
came during the nation's ultimate test, the Great Depression of the
1930s. During that period the camera emerged from the idealized
situations of the studio and entered the reality of the streets. Mag-

azines began to make more use of "realistic" photography, and photographers developed styles and approaches that better fitted the harsh realities of the times. By 1935 the move toward honest documentation was having an impact on the information agencies of the federal government. That year a group was brought together, dedicated to the use of powerful still photographs to show the nation its rural problems. Later the same group would broaden its interests to include virtually all aspects of American life, the strengths as well as the weaknesses. By the time the agency was dissolved, in the early days of World War II, it had played a key role in conditioning the esthetic tastes of the nation to the documentary style, while at the same time it had created a tremendously valuable record of the age of the Great Depression.

The following pages will attempt to describe in some detail the birth, productive years, and the death of the "historical section" of the Farm Security Administration (which was called the Resettlement Administration in the early days). Because this agency was to a great extent the product of its director's energy and talent, the focus is on the personality of Roy Stryker, chief of the historical section. Like any large creative project, however, the work of the historical section was an amalgamation of many fine minds; therefore an effort has been made to introduce the principal photographers who contributed to the total documentary effort. As remarkable as the staff was the fact that the historical section functioned within the context of a government bureau. This meant that there were established certain limitations and responsibilities that formed a fascinating backdrop for the group's activities.

The book concerns itself with the development of the documentary style by the historical section photographers, the uses made of the pictures, and the long-term influence of the project. It is not proposed to spend more than the necessary minimum of time with federal agricultural policies, nor is a detailed criticism of photographic styles within the scope of this study. The real object is to delineate as precisely as possible how such a tremendous outpouring of talent could come about in a depression, in a farm agency of the federal government that employed a delicate mixture of talented people of different views and approaches.

Finally, it seems necessary to point out that the agency's historical section was not the only group in the government that used photographs. The Department of the Interior, the Department of Agriculture, and in fact 70 percent of all federal agencies used pictures in one way or another during the 1930s.[1] Three factors distinguished the work of the historical section. First, its staff was intensely professional. FSA photographers were never hired because they needed work. They were hired because they possessed real ability to capture fine pictures. Second, the FSA group was committed from the beginning to a policy of total truthfulness. Their pictures were often used as propaganda for the agency, but it was propaganda in the best sense—that is, the photographs focused attention on real problems and hinted at real solutions. And because the people who worked for Roy Stryker were individuals and were respected as such, many photographs were taken that did not support, either directly or indirectly, the work of the agency. Third, the historical section was distinguished by its sense of history. Other agencies might make thousands of routine photographic records of their programs in action, but the historical section photographers sought to capture their agency's work against the backdrop of the entire national life.[2] Instead of focusing merely on poor farmers, its personnel caught the relationships between rural poverty and improper land use, the decline of the small farming community and the growth of urban blight. Because the staff had this sense of history, the photographs were saved to constitute a permanent national treasure.

Roy Stryker and his people had set out to document a decade. Their story is one that has proven endlessly fascinating to this writer. It is hoped that retelling it will shed light on some aspects of the creative processes.

Contents

PORTRAIT
OF A
DECADE

I

A New Force in Education and Photography: Roy Emerson Stryker

West of Montrose, Colorado, a narrow road runs out across the flat toward the mesa that dominates the valley. Along that road, sometime after the turn of the century, a small boy astride a donkey inched across the flatland. Both were preoccupied, the donkey with the dust at his feet and the boy with a book in which he was totally absorbed. Neither noticed the heavy four-horse freight wagon that came rumbling up behind them. For a few seconds, the driver waited for the pair to react to his presence. Then, in exasperation at their slow pace, he shouted: "You Goddamned little upstart! Get out of the road! What are you trying to do, you silly little bastard! Are you trying to read!"[1] The man's attitude was typical of western Colorado residents in those days and the boy was accustomed to it. Roy Emerson Stryker merely shrugged and laughed as he pulled aside to let the man pass. The West was his country. He loved his books and read as often as possible, but he loved the earthy, rough-and-tumble ways of his region, too.

Stryker came from a line of people who combined a love of learning with a strong feeling for the soil. His father had farmed in Kansas during the height of the Populist movement and had felt the awakening of interest in books and economic theories that had so gripped that area.[2] He had brought his family, his love of books, and a certain idealistic radicalism to Montrose in search of better farm land. He found only the harsh "dobie" hills to the northeast of town. Living was not easy but the Strykers got along. The father dabbled in politics and small business ventures, and found enough money to provide the seven children with as much education as they could absorb. By the time Roy was in school, an older brother was working as a public school administrator in

Kansas and was sending the younger children all sorts of books. Stryker later recalled poring over everything from handbooks of the United States Department of Agriculture to a history of Rome.[3] At the same time, a steady diet of hard ranch work assured that his hands would not grow too soft.

In May, 1912, Roy graduated from high school and sought more education, an unusual thing to do if one lived in western Colorado in those days.[4] Encouragement came from the high school principal, who also doubled as the chemistry teacher. Stryker's grades had been above average in all subjects, but particularly high in chemistry and the sciences. He had been given the run of the chemistry laboratory and his interests had bloomed.[5] The choice of college seemed obvious. The Colorado School of Mines, one of the nation's finest technical schools, lay just over the mountains at Golden, waiting to be conquered. It looked like the easy and natural course of events, but higher learning was to come hard for Roy. During his first year at college, he found himself plagued by weak eyes and low funds. By the end of the spring term in 1913, it was clear that his eyes, which had never been really strong, were not bearing the strain of college work.

A very discouraged Roy Stryker returned home in the summer of 1913 to try his hand at the only other thing he knew, ranching. With one of his brothers as a partner, he took up homestead land in the highlands above Montrose, and for the next several years his address was the Uncompaghre Valley.[6] Summers found the young men fattening cattle on the Indian lands near their ranch, while winters usually drove them out of the highlands to work in one of the mines in the Montrose area. Hard work, healthy living, and few opportunities for reading seemed to agree with Roy and slowly his eyesight improved.

By the time the United States was drawn into World War I, Stryker was sun-tanned and hard. He was also ready for a change. Along with thousands of others he "joined up," enlisting in the infantry. Even in the anonymous role of a foot soldier, Stryker made his mark in his own highly individualistic style. He seemed to have an instinctive feel for the language of the military. The rough speech of the range and mine were as much a part of him as were his thick glasses. (In fact, during his career in Washington, Stryker would become somewhat of a legend for his pungent turn of phrase.) During basic training he so impressed his commanding officer with the beauty and artistry of his swearing that he was given the job of teaching the untrained city boys of the platoon the finer points of unconventional language so that they

4

George and Ellen Stryker,
Roy Stryker's parents.
Roy E. Stryker and
Phyllis Stryker Wilson

Roy Stryker's brothers
and mother. Will, Arthur,
Delbert, Roy (in front).
Roy E. Stryker and
Phyllis Stryker Wilson

would have something to shout during bayonet drill. But even in the army, the two sides of his character remained. He gravitated naturally to the better educated, more intellectual men in the unit. He made friends with a professor of botany. Another close friend was a dentist; several others were school teachers. In contact with these people, Stryker grew increasingly restless.[7] His unit spent nine months in France, but even while overseas he was planning a new start in education as soon as he returned home. Everyone seemed to agree that Columbia University in New York was a fine choice. Very well, Roy would simply remain on the East Coast when he returned and attend Columbia.

As often happens the plans of the young man and those of the United States Army failed to mesh. The army had inducted Roy Emerson Stryker at Fort Leavenworth, Kansas, and it was going to bring him back to where it had found him. As a result, in the late winter of 1919, Roy found himself back in the West.[8] The records of the Colorado School of Mines show that he reentered in February, 1920, in time to begin the second term that year. This time his eyes proved adequate and it seemed that higher education was at last within reach. But there were decisions to be made. There was the ranch up in the Uncompaghre Valley and letters from home told of a need there.

That summer Stryker went through a kind of confirmation. After the school term was over he "went up on the mountain" for a last look, pressing his favorite horse and several dogs into service as company. The time passed swiftly, for Stryker loved the mountains, but when the trip was over, he knew that he would not be coming back to them. Agricultural prices had broken and the ranching business was entering a period of decline. Wartime needs had pushed farm prices to a record high in 1917 and 1918, but by 1920 Europe was recovering and American farm products were not so badly needed. Stryker saw the downward trend in prices and felt that he could not spend the rest of his life tied to "the price of hay and the price of beef."[9]

In order to earn money for the next school year, he worked on a nearby sheep ranch. There, at a Fourth-of-July picnic, one face seemed to stand out from the crowd. Alice Frasier warmed to the rather gruff advances of this young man who always seemed to be in such a hurry. Roy would later describe the courtship in this way: "One of the old gals that was in high school came up for the Fourth-of-July. To make the story short, I decided I was in love. I thought I had been a woman hater. I decided to get married and I needed a wife."[10]

6

Stryker during the early
ranching years.
*Roy E. Stryker and
Phyllis Stryker Wilson*

What woman could resist such gallant eloquence! During the next year, Roy and Alice continued to see each other while he studied at Golden and Alice taught at a public school nearby. That winter was a time of learning and mental growth for them both. It was during this time that Roy became interested in economics and social problems.

When time, money, and the weather permitted, Roy and Alice liked to go into Denver, where a number of their friends lived and worked. A close circle of socially concerned young people developed around the personality of a young minister named George Collins. Collins was interested in the ideas of Walter Rauschenbusch and was deeply committed to that minister's advocacy of a "social gospel." Stimulated by Collins' ideas, Roy and Alice began to work with boys' clubs in the city, gaining an awareness of urban problems that neither had possessed before. Stryker later remembered: "I read the *New Republic* and I saw the *Nation,* and I read a lot of Rauschenbusch. I read a lot of things and my life was changing rapidly."[11] The group often met in Collins' home to discuss their new ideas. What began as weekly sessions soon became Monday-Wednesday-Friday affairs. In the course of these sessions, Roy mentioned his earlier interest in Columbia University, and Collins encouraged him to consider going back East. The minister had contacts in New York and knew people at the Union Theological Seminary. As Collins talked about the pace and excitement of life in the city, Stryker's appetite was whetted. More than ever before, it seemed necessary to go East.

As always in such decisions, the problem of money was a factor. Roy had a small disability check coming from the government because he had contracted a serious case of influenza during the war, but this was hardly adequate to cover even transportation expenses. Alice had saved a little from her teaching, but the aggregate still fell far short of their needs. The only other asset was the ranch. Roy tried to sell it during the summer of 1921. A neighbor agreed to take the land at a fair price, and for a while it seemed as though all of the problems would work themselves out. Roy and Alice were married in September and were preparing to head East when trouble struck again. The year 1921 had proven to be even worse for agricultural prices than 1920, and the neighbor who had agreed to take the ranch was forced to default. There were no other buyers.[12] At this point George Collins offered to write the people at Union Settlement House in New York. Perhaps some sort of social work might be available.[13] Stryker was so taken with the idea that he bundled Alice on a train for New York without even waiting for an answer. It was a "leap of faith" in the classic sense. The whole idea seemed so right to Roy that he was sure nothing could go wrong. Alice reserved judgment.

The trip East was the nearest thing to a honeymoon that Alice Stryker would ever know. Although their money was stretching thin, Roy insisted that they see Niagara Falls because that was what people were supposed to do on their honeymoon, but even there Roy was nervous and anxious to move on. New York City was where he wanted to be and New York City was where he was going to be. The two young people arrived in New York completely unprepared for city living. Roy almost became involved in a fight with the first porter who tried to carry his luggage: "Take your hands off that bag, God damn it! That's *my* bag!"[14] But, of course, they had the tip from George Collins to fall back on. Accordingly Roy went to see Max Nelson, the director of the settlement house, and asked whether some sort of job was available. As it turned out, Nelson had received Collins' letter and was expecting them. At least they could be sure of a roof over their heads. For the next year Roy and Alice Stryker were employees of the Union Settlement House.

The settlement house was a project of the Union Theological Seminary. In order to be eligible for permanent employment and lodging there, one had to be a registered student at Union Seminary. Roy was not able to register, because he did not have the required bachelor of arts degree. Therefore, because she had acquired her bachelor's degree before her marriage, patient and long-suffering Alice was duly enrolled as a theological student while Roy went on with the original plan of studying at Columbia University. In the time left over from their studies, the two young people earned their room and board by working with the children who came to the settlement house. These labors earned them one meal a day (supper) and a room with a bathroom that doubled as a kitchen. This was a time of excitement and hardship for them. "That town hit us like a ton of bricks,"[15] Roy would later recall. Roy's deep interest in and compassion for people was piqued by the sights and sounds of the slums around the settlement house. For him this was a period of widening horizons, with no regrets for the comparatively good life that had been left behind in Colorado. It was also a time for finding himself at the university.

During that first year a lasting friendship was formed between Stryker and his instructor in economics. It was in many ways a strange, rather stand-offish relationship, for Rexford Guy Tugwell always avoided personal contacts. Even so the professor

was evidently impressed with his unpolished western student.
Stryker's recollection of the first encounter seems to sum up their
association:

> My first year up there I ran into Tugwell. He was giving courses in
> Utopian Socialism and various things. I haven't forgotten yet the time
> I had to write a paper.
>
> He said, "If I don't like it you will get a D and if it isn't on time you'll
> get a D."
>
> So I was late. And I got my paper back and the note on it said,
> "You're late but I'm giving you an A minus, but I am going to give you
> an A because it's typed and that's progress."[16]

Tugwell was more than a stimulating teacher of economics;
he was a man who could teach Stryker much about visual aids
as an adjunct to learning. Tugwell believed strongly in descriptive
economics. He felt that it was important for students to have
visual contact with the economic institutions they were studying.
What did a bank look like? What did a cotton farm look like? How
did it differ from a rice farm? By firing questions such as these
at his class, Tugwell increasingly piqued Stryker's thoughts about
the process of visual identification. In this area, Tugwell was
not alone. There was much interest in the use of pictures, graphs,
and other visual aids among the university's faculty. Professor
Harry Carman, head of the Department of History, was a great
admirer of the *Pageant of America* series, a multivolume picture
history of the United States published by Yale University. When
Stryker showed interest in this area, Carman loaned him the key
to his office and allowed him to spend as much time as he wished
with the books.[17] John Coss, a professor of economics and government who taught a section of the required problems course called
"Contemporary Civilization," added another important dimension
to Stryker's thinking and his later teaching. It was he who encouraged Stryker to get out and see specific things for himself.
Coss loved to take students on day-long outings to observe various
facets of American life. On almost any weekend when the weather
permitted, Coss could be found in a museum or other educational
institution with a group of students in tow, firing questions at
them. "Do you see that painting? What does it remind you of?
Does it tell you anything about the period it was done in? Think!"[18]
These trips became a cherished part of Stryker's education and
a part that he spent a great deal of time passing on to others.

At the end of the first year, Roy and Alice left the Union Settlement House and moved closer to the campus. They had rented an
inexpensive apartment, and they had learned to support them-

selves by doing odd jobs around the university. Roy discovered
that he and Alice had a talent for making graphs and that there
were professors who were willing to pay good money to see their
theoretical ideas and calculations reduced to understandable di-
mensions.[19] Besides Roy was somewhat disillusioned with life at
the settlement house. It seemed to have an unreal, visionary air
about it. The staff members were trying to help individuals, but
they were powerless to do anything about the system that was
causing the trouble. "I was basically a radical. I was basically from
a socialist home," he later remembered.[20] Life outside the settlement was certainly more precarious, but it was also more satisfying.

After three years at Columbia, Stryker had received his bachelor's degree in economics and was in the process of completing his
master of arts degree. By this time he was so well entrenched in
the Department of Economics that it was felt he could be trusted
with some teaching chores. Columbia University records show
that in May, 1924, Roy Emerson Stryker was appointed Assistant
in Economics. It was to be a one-year appointment with a salary
of $1,000 a year.[21] In this job he functioned as a teaching assis-
tant. The professor responsible for the course was to lecture twice
a week and Stryker was to conduct the "third hour" or quiz section. Most graduate students who taught these sections simply
met their classes, asked if there were any questions, and perhaps
led a discussion on some problem that the professor had raised
during his lecture. This is what the administration had expected
Stryker to do, but he had other plans.

Stryker had been assigned to assist in a course on labor problems; very well, he would take the students to a few labor meetings
and let them observe labor problems—from the bottom up. The
idea took hold. The young men from Columbia found the involvement in the actual dynamics of the labor movement a fascinating
experience. The union men responded to their interest by inviting
them to join the ranks of a picket line, which they did. Soon even
graduate students were coming along on Stryker's "trips." The idea
grew so popular that the crowds became unwieldy, and he had to
be cautioned that the professor who taught the course (a woman)
was becoming a little jealous.[22] Jealousies aside, the faculty had to
realize that Stryker had hit upon a viable technique for teaching.
For the next several years, he held the position of Assistant in
Economics and continued to take his students on trips around the
city. At the same time, he pursued his own graduate studies.

It was during Stryker's first year as a student assistant that

Tugwell called him into his office and announced: "We're doing a
book called *American Economic Life* and I want it illustrated.
We'll pay you for the job or you can be a joint author."[23] The
book, which was being put together by Tugwell and Thomas Munro, was expected to fill the need for a basic text in the freshman
course "Contemporary Civilization." The whole concept of a
course in contemporary civilization was quite new in 1924. Columbia University had been experimenting with the course for
about six years at this point and had found it both difficult and
extremely stimulating for students and instructors. A battery
of some twenty young teachers had been involved in the work.
Among these men were representatives of the fields of economics,
history, literature, and education. Included were some of the most
able men on the faculty. From Tugwell to the then unknown Roy
F. Nichols, these men worked hard to make the experiment in
interdisciplinary teaching a success.

The book itself was a broad-ranging project, designed to ac-
quaint the student with urban and rural poverty, labor-manage-
ment relations, production and distribution, and other problems of
modern society. Beginning with clear yet sophisticated definitions
of poor, comfortable, and rich standards of living, the book would
go on to discuss the various philosophies of distribution and their
relative effects on society. Theory would be included. From Adam
Smith to Marx, the philosophers would be allowed to have their
say. Always, however, theory was to be adjunct to commercial and
social reality so far as the authors could identify it.[24]

The invitation to Stryker to be included in the project was flattering, and he immediately decided that he would prefer the long-
term gains of authorship to any short-term monetary gains that
might come from doing the project for a salary. So it was decided.
Roy Stryker was to handle the selection and editing of all illustrative material for the new textbook. For the next year, the book
project occupied all of his spare time. Thousands of pictures were
gathered, gazed at, winnowed, rejected, and loved.

The process of gathering illustrations for *American Economic
Life* was the beginning of Stryker's education in the use of photographs. He quickly discovered that they were not being widely
used by the popular media to illustrate social problems or economic points of view. In fact the magazines of the day, *Vogue, Vanity
Fair,* and others used photographs to present an idealized view of
life as it ought to be, rather than life as it was. The top magazine
photographers were extremely skilled technicians and often sensitive artists, but they tended to see the photograph as an end in
itself, a thing of beauty with no message beyond its own perfec-

tion. Edward Steichen's famous high-fashion photographs in *Vanity Fair* perhaps epitomized the era. He and the Californian Edward Weston, whose seascapes, twisted trees, and finely detailed closeups revealed an intense personal response to the beauties of nature, indicated that American photographers were capable of high art and sensitivity. Their pictures were beautiful but they were not what Stryker needed. He needed pictures that were visually strong but that also possessed a social consciousness. Given the generally escapist tone of most of the publication media during the 1920s, such pictures would not be easy to locate. Yet a tradition of photographs with social awareness did exist, although it was a small tradition and somewhat removed from the mainstream of the photography of the day.

Since the beginning of photography in the United States, some picture makers had recognized the value of their work as a record of their times. Mathew Brady's portraits of famous men and women of the 1840s and 1850s and his later pictures of Civil War battlefields were certainly documents.[25] Jacob Riis's book, *How the Other Half Lives*, had made use of dozens of Riis's own photographs of slums in order to bludgeon home his message on the evils of poverty in American cities. The book, published in 1890, had mobilized public opinion behind programs to improve the New York slums as no other method could have.[26] Still later, the work of Lewis Hine had exposed the evils of child labor in the factories. Hine, a former schoolteacher, had taken his cameras into the glass works and textile mills and had photographed children and their mothers working under the most intolerable conditions. In 1908 he had left the classroom to work for Frank Kellogg, reform editor and publisher of *Charities and Commons* (later known as the *Survey* and still later as *Survey Graphic*.) Hine's cameras had provided incontrovertible evidence that some businessmen were habitually exploiting children and women. The pictures that he took were important documents, but they were also carefully composed, powerful photographs, capable of standing on their own merit.[27]

Although Hine and Riis were turning their cameras on social problems, most photographers preferred to explore their own inner vision. Alfred Stieglitz, Margaret Kasebier, and the other "serious" photographers of the Progressive Era did not see any need to become involved in social movements. Their search was for abstract beauty.[28] The men who used cameras as tools for social understanding were left out of the mainstream of salon and magazine photography. This tradition of idealization in pictures continued into the 1920s and, indeed, became even more domi-

nant. As Stryker searched the magazines and the files of the photographic agencies, he became increasingly aware that photographs
were not being used as effectively as they could be. Social problems existed in plenty during the mid-1920s, but the camera was
not being used to point them out.

Eventually Stryker found the photographs that he needed. Ironically, however, many had been taken almost twenty years earlier,
by Lewis Hine himself. Of the two hundred and fifteen illustrations used in the book, more than seventy were photographs by
the aging crusader. Both Tugwell and Stryker had known and
admired his work in the *Survey* and other socially oriented publications. The great documentary photographer and the young teaching assistant became good friends during the weeks and months
that *American Economic Life* was in preparation. Hine would
come to Columbia with great armloads of pictures drawn from
his vast experience in the areas of child labor, poverty, and industrial photography.[29] Did the book need pictures of representative
immigrant types? Hine could present examples showing typically
Slavic, male and female; typically Nordic, male and female, and so
on by the dozens. Did the authors need some method of contrast-
ing substandard with standard and high-standard housing? Hine
had at one time or another taken exactly the photographs needed.
So complete were his files that it was never necessary to send him
out to take a specific picture. If a search of other sources did not
turn up a required illustration, Hine could usually be counted
upon to rummage around in his own holdings and come up with
what was needed.

In addition to the work by Lewis Hine, Stryker could fall back
on "stock pictures" from the files of such agencies as Ewing-
Galloway. Also specific industries were often willing to provide
illustrations of their own activities. From Ford, for example, came
pictures of a production line. As a result the finished book must
still stand today as one of the most lavishly illustrated economic
texts of all time.

The first edition of *American Economic Life* was a privately
printed manual solely for the use of Columbia students. It came
out in the spring of 1925 and contained no illustrations.[30] But
by the summer of that year however, the illustrated edition was
published by Harcourt, Brace and Company. Now Stryker was an
author: his name was on a book. But more important, he had discovered his great love in life. The experience of hunting pictures
to illustrate abstract ideas had been the most exciting thing he
had ever done. He could not let the matter drop: the fascination
was too much. Almost before the first published edition was in

the bookstores, Stryker was at work on a second version. For the next five years, until 1930, he continued to work as a student assistant and to hunt pictures for the book, always pressing for better use of photographs, more sophisticated layout, and better quality pictures. The second published version (officially the third edition) showed the care that Stryker had lavished upon it. The fine work of Lewis Hine remained, but many of the stock pictures from Ewing-Galloway and other agencies had been replaced. One significant new name appeared among the photographic credits. Margaret Bourke-White made a large contribution to the later edition. Several of her excellent pictures of industry were included. In the process of utilizing the work of the then relatively unknown girl, Stryker had several opportunities to meet and work with her. His education in the use of photographs and the direction of photographers continued.[31]

It should be kept in mind that, throughout the period of Stryker's employment by Columbia University, he was primarily a teacher. The work on the book was done after hours and on weekends for the most part. Stryker loved to teach. He enjoyed challenging young minds and watching them open up to new concepts. In May, 1929, university records show that he was appointed Instructor in Economics and that his salary was raised to $3,000 a year.[32] This was not so much a reward for academic excellence (for it was by now becoming clear that Roy was not going to complete work on a Ph.D.) as it was a recognition of his effectiveness as a teacher of freshman and sophomore courses. Roy continued to be a stimulating classroom teacher but, even more, his trips out into the city became his primary mode of instruction. This technique, which John Coss had begun and Stryker had perfected, became such a popular option that Tugwell, who was by this time head of the Department of Economics, suggested that the trips be institutionalized:

> And one day he [Tugwell] said, "you know, why don't we offer a course here—why don't we give a sort of laboratory course in conjunction with our 'Contemporary Civilization,' give it in the sophomore year —economics and government?" So it was organized. . . . They had a choice. There were certain requirements they had to go to—and this was right up my alley because I could see more of the city and I loved it, and I didn't have to use brains that I didn't have. I didn't have to be the bright scholar. And I taught right along as I had always taught.[33]

From 1929 until 1935 the organization and planning of the trips for the "Contemporary Civilization" laboratories consumed a large part of Stryker's professional attention. Student groups were sent to banks, museums, slaughterhouses, and slums. In fact the student could choose his six trips from some thirty options. One man who was a student from 1931 to 1935 remembered his trips as being a high point in the educational process at the university. Arthur Rothstein, who later became one of the top photographers for the Farm Security Administration, was a chemistry major, but the sophomore laboratory course in economics and government so impressed him that he never forgot it.[34] Actually, because it made him a better observer, the course undoubtedly affected his whole career. Rothstein remembered that the driving force behind the success of the trips was the personality of Roy Stryker. He was always there in the background, questioning, probing, forcing students to think.

The years at Columbia passed well for Roy and Alice Stryker, but toward the end certain frustrations appear to have developed. The work on *American Economic Life* was finished and there were not any strong prospects for a fourth edition. Stryker was teaching first-year economics and helping Tugwell with some upper division classes, both of which activities he enjoyed. There were always the trips around the city, which were an immense source of pleasure, but without a good excuse to look at pictures and to use pictures for teaching, Stryker would never be completely happy again. Outside the university the depression was deepening and he disliked his own noninvolvement. Like many other Americans in this period, he felt a deep need to do something, almost anything, to relieve his own frustration over the economic crisis. Finally it must be noted that a confrontation occurred between Stryker and Tugwell over the subject of Stryker's academic advancement.

The date of the conversation is impossible to determine today, but it must have been in the early 1930s that Tugwell finally forced the issue. "Roy," he asked, "do you want a doctorate?" "Well, no, I don't know that I do, Rex. I don't know that I want one." "Well, damn it, do what you want to and forget it!"[35]

Stryker would later remember this exchange vividly for it was a blow finally to recognize that he was not basically an academic person; yet Tugwell, in his harshness, had not intended to be unkind. His interest was in helping Stryker find his own niche. In a long walk by the Hudson, Roy turned the whole conversation over in his mind. Tugwell had said, "Do what you want to," but what did he want to do? He loved to teach and he loved to use pictures to make his points, but how could the two elements be brought together? In time events brought the answer, but not without some searching on his part.

II
Changing
Political Winds

When the depression struck the cities of America in late 1929, it brought no startling news to the farms. Rural people in large sections were hardly aware of a change, for they had already known hard times for almost a decade. The falling farm prices that had convinced Roy Stryker that the life of a rancher was not for him had hit agriculture a widespread blow. By 1921 the war credits that this country had extended to our European allies were pretty well used up and, with Congress in a frugal mood, no more were forthcoming. The nations of Europe were forced to fall back on their own resources and to cultivate new sources for their farm needs. As the foreign markets disappeared, domestic prices began to disintegrate. The farmer began to suffer.

No one had expected trouble. During the war years farmers had stretched themselves to their financial and physical limits. Food Administrator Herbert Hoover in the nation's capital had called for more wheat and more corn and more beef; the men who considered themselves the "backbone of the nation" would deliver. As an added incentive to patriotism, wartime prices had been higher than anybody could remember.[1] In all sections of the country, farmers had borrowed money, bought new equipment, opened up vast new areas to the plow, and expanded their operations. Naturally, with the buoyant optimism that has always characterized American farmers, they expected the good times to roll on—and on.

The downturn in 1920 caught thousands of farmers unprepared. No one seemed to understand why times had suddenly turned bad or to know what to do about the situation. The government raised tariff barriers in an effort to protect United States farm produce, but this move proved worse than useless because many farmers depended on exports to provide their profit margin.[2] In effect we were denying our European neighbors the right to sell goods in

17

this country through the use of tariff barriers, yet we expected them to continue to buy our own farm products at wartime prices. This sort of shortsighted thinking and lack of planning led to an agricultural slump that lasted throughout the decade. Cotton prices, for example, fell 60 percent between 1920 and 1921.[3] In the South sharecroppers were singing:

> Eleven cent cotton, forty cent meat,
> How in the Hell can a poor man eat?
> Pray for the sunshine, cause it's gonna rain.
> Things gittin worse—driven all insane;
> Built a nice barn, painted it brown;
> Lightenin came along and burnt it down.
>
> No use talkin! any man's beat
> with 'leven cent cotton and forty cent meat.

Other farm prices followed suit and at the same time the costs of running a profitable farm began to increase. It was no longer possible to make a good living with forty acres and a mule (if indeed it ever had been possible). More and more farmers were finding it necessary to mechanize, to use tractors and multirow equipment. All of this required money, and the need came at the precise time that most farmers were finding it difficult to obtain money. As a result the natural tendency among American farmers was to maintain as much land in production as humanly possible and farm it intensively—and often carelessly.[4]

All of these factors—too much land in cultivation, poor trade conditions, and new expenses—are easily documented. In human terms, however, they meant that the gap between the quality of life on the farm and life in the city was widening dangerously during the decade of the so-called "roaring twenties." The established farmer faced the specter of foreclosure, for rural banks were usually in a weak position and thus unable to give extensions on loans when needed. In many cases, unable to meet the obligations he had incurred during the patriotic flush of war, the landowner was forced to join the landless ranks of tenant farmers.

The slow but steady increase in tenancy during the 1920s posed a serious threat to the stability of rural institutions. When a man does not own the land he works, there is a tendency to mine the soil, ripping from it all of the cash crops that he can get. Whether he rents or farms on shares, the fact remains that the tenant is not ultimately responsible for the land. He does not own it. If it becomes worn out, he expects to move on. Add to this situation a burden of debt and the pressures on man and land become re-

Plantation owner, Clarks-
dale, Mississippi, 1936.
Dorothea Lange.

lentless. The tenant who is in debt must squeeze the last bit of
cash from the land. He cannot afford to think of fertilizers or
special soil-building techniques. The manuals from the Department of Agriculture may suggest crop rotation or the planting
and turning under of nitrate-rich grasses, but the farmer cannot
even consider such things. He must make a crop and pay his bills
in town. As a result, after a few years, the land declines in fertility and the farmer finds himself in worse shape than before. To
compound the problems faced by the tenant, the use of more
mechanical equipment in the twenties meant that he was less and
less needed; thus, the option of moving somewhere else and finding another farm was less and less available.

One way or another, most farmers lost ground during the decade
before the depression. In 1929 there were about 1,700,000 farms
in this country which yielded a gross income of less than $600
for the entire year. A few more than 900,000 yielded less than
$400. In the worst areas, such as the cutover lands of Wisconsin
and large parts of the South where the sharecrop system was common, almost 400,000 farms grossed less than $250 each for the
entire year's labor. These figures represented about 7,700,000
people who were living so far below the poverty line that normal
socioeconomic definitions were almost meaningless.[5]

The farmer and his representatives in government fought back,
but during the twenties theirs was a losing battle. The high tariffs
that helped to dry up foreign markets are an example of farm-
belt influence. Many farmers mistakenly favored the protection
that tariffs could give. Few possessed the sophistication to think
the problem through completely and see that high tariffs were
more likely to hurt than help them. Even more important for
future developments were the battles over such farm legislation as
the McNary-Haugen bill and the export debenture plan.

The McNary-Haugen plan, first devised by George Peek and
Hugh Johnson of the Moline Plow Company and presented to
Congress in 1923 by Senator Charles L. McNary and Representative Gilbert N. Haugen of Iowa, proposed to pay farmers a stabi-
lized fair price for nonperishable staples based on the average of
the last ten years before World War I. What goods our own national economy could not absorb were to be dumped overseas. Any
losses incurred by this action were to be divided among the farmers.[6] The plan passed Congress twice, only to be vetoed each time
by Republican Presidents who thought nothing of protecting industry, but who considered any program for the benefit of agriculture dangerously socialistic. The export debenture plan was a

West Main Street,
Norfolk, Virginia, 1941.
John Vachon.

Abandoned farmhouse,
Ward County, North
Dakota. John Vachon.

rather complicated scheme to encourage exporters to handle farm goods and assure their profits. A classic example of the "trickle down" economics of the Republican era, the plan had the support of powerful conservative farm organizations such as the National Grange. The idea was to subsidize exporters in the naïve expectation that the exporters would then pass their new-found wealth down to the farmers in the form of higher prices.[7]

McNary-Haugen was vetoed. Export debenture never even got that far. Both served a purpose, however. From about 1923 until the early 1930s, these plans and their advocates continued to remind the country of the problems that farmers faced. The discussion of various ideas for government programs to aid the farmer served to condition the ordinary citizen (both rural and urban) to the notion that sooner or later the government was going to have to become directly involved in the farm problem. This meant that by the time Franklin D. Roosevelt took office in 1933, two important factors had helped to create a political climate conducive to legislative and governmental experimentation. The depressed conditions in agriculture meant that a majority of farmers were ready to go along with almost any plan that offered hope; and the long years of rural agitation for government programs had accustomed people to look to Washington as the agency of their deliverance.

One of the people most interested in experimental programs to aid the rural poor was Rexford Tugwell, Roy Stryker's mentor at Columbia University. Cool, witty, urbane, the last sort of man anyone would ever expect to see on a farm, Tugwell was nevertheless one of this country's best-informed experts on agricultural problems. As a boy Tugwell had lived in a farming community. His father had engaged in a number of agricultural businesses in upstate New York, among them commercial fruit and dairy farms, but the Tugwells had been primarily businessmen.[8] Rexford was sent to the University of Pennsylvania because it had a good business college.[9] Clearly the elder Tugwell expected his son to return to the family enterprises in Niagara County. Things did not work out according to plan. Young Rex came under the spell of Simon Patten, a brilliant economist who believed deeply in man's ability to change economic institutions and thereby improve himself.[10] In his sophomore year, Tugwell fell in love with economics, and that was the end of any serious consideration of returning to the family businesses.

By 1916 Tugwell had a master's degree and was teaching economics at the University of Pennsylvania.[11] In 1920 he moved to

FSA borrower and wife, cutover area of Itasca
County, Minnesota, 1941. John Vachon.

Church at Wounded
Knee, South Dakota,
1940. John Vachon.
Library of Congress

Columbia University, where he found himself in the stimulating company of men such as John Coss (the professor who taught Stryker to love trips into the city) and John Dewey, the philosopher of Pragmatism.[12] At Columbia Tugwell taught all sorts of courses in the general area of economics, but gradually he became more and more interested in special rural problems. Given the fact that American farmers probably suffered more, economically, in the twenties than any other group, the reason for his interest becomes clear. Here was where the help was needed.

After he received his Ph.D. degree in 1922, Tugwell's promotion to associate professor in 1926 seemed to insure that he could count on a long and successful academic career.[13] In all probability he would have been willing to remain a teacher had events not moved him out of the academic world and into the political sphere. But those who knew him well were aware that he was not entirely satisfied. One Columbia graduate remembers Tugwell as having little to do with his students. The young professor seemed to prefer that assistants such as Stryker handle actual dealings with students, while reserving his own energies for research and writing.[14] Tugwell's research led him to the conclusion that the country was being badly mismanaged. The depression was worsening during the early 1930s and the Hoover administration seemed paralyzed. Nobody seemed to understand that the worst of the economic troubles were caused by lack of purchasing power among farmers and working-class people. It all seemed so simple to Tugwell, yet nobody was listening.[15]

An opportunity to speak his piece came in March, 1932. Raymond Moley, his next-door neighbor and colleague on the faculty of Columbia University, met him one cold, blustery morning as both men were leaving their apartments and asked if Tugwell could give him some advice. Moley, who had been writing speeches for Franklin D. Roosevelt, then governor of New York, felt the need to talk to someone with a thorough grounding in economics. Governor Roosevelt, already a definite presidential possibility, needed new ideas about what could be done about the depression. In particular new ideas were needed about the farm problem. Could Tugwell help? Tugwell was both pleased and excited by the prospect: "I really needed little persuasion. The truth is I felt myself deeply involved in the strangulation of the economy. Those who had the power to lead were not taking the reasonable way out. And this was the only opening I had had—besides talking and writing—to a means of doing anything about it."[16]

Tugwell went to Albany, visited the governor, and talked about his ideas for recovery. As a result, he found himself one of three close advisors to Roosevelt. Raymond Moley helped write speeches and provided advice in the area of law. Adolf Berle, another member of the Columbia faculty, provided help in the area of business recovery. Tugwell's responsibilities included programs of a general economic nature and especially for agricultural recovery. These three men were to be the prospective candidate's "idea men." Roosevelt could call on them for data and theories that he could not find time to develop for himself. Within a few weeks, New York *Times* reporter James M. Kieran had given the group the name the "brains trust" and the phrase stuck.[17]

So Tugwell became a "brain truster" and began to spend a great deal of time with the governor. Throughout the next year, academic duties at the university were more and more given over to other teachers as he increasingly became involved in Roosevelt's political career. It was an exciting, satisfying, yet frustrating time for Tugwell. He knew that Roosevelt was essentially a patrician reformer, yet there was just a chance, if he could make his ideas clear, that Roosevelt could be made to understand that the times demanded something that went beyond mere reform. Tugwell favored government planning for all parts of the economy. He was an unabashed federalist who sought a far greater role for the government than even the New Deal was to bring.[18] During the spring of 1932, Tugwell traveled with Roosevelt, wrote speeches for him, had long conversations with him, and helped him to clarify his ideas. People who met and talked with the prospective candidate during this period were consistently impressed with his knowledge of economic problems. Much of this information was coming from the "brains trust."

After the Democratic National Convention nominated Roosevelt for President, Tugwell continued to act as an advisor and aid in speech writing. He played a key part in several major decisions during the campaign. It was Tugwell, for example, who saw the value of a new agricultural program proposed by Professor Milburn L. Wilson of the University of Montana. Called by the musty name, "voluntary domestic allotment," Wilson's idea called for government price supports, but this aid was to be linked to a reduction of crops. Tugwell believed that the idea had all the requisites for success. Wilson even suggested that acceptance of government aid be made the responsibility of local boards, so that the program would have the necessary modicum of "home rule." Excitedly Tugwell brought Wilson's ideas to Roosevelt and explained them in detail.[19] A few months later, the Agricultural Adjustment

Act embodied voluntary domestic allotment as the central theme
in the government's farm program.

When the campaign was over and Roosevelt was the new President, Tugwell was so involved in the national decision-making
process that it would have been unthinkable for him to return to
full-time teaching. He was consulted on the appointment of the
secretary of agriculture and suggested Henry Wallace, a Republican newspaper editor from Iowa. He had been impressed with the
Wallace family and the leadership they had provided in farm affairs for some time, and he succeeded in "selling" the administration on the appointment.[20] Wallace, in turn, seems to have genuinely wanted the young eastern professor as a close advisor; thus,
Tugwell became assistant secretary of agriculture.[21] The appointment was a good one for Tugwell. It lacked the political pressures
that the top cabinet position carried with it, yet there was real
power to be exercised. When major decisions were to be made,
Tugwell would be in on them.

After the inauguration Tugwell moved to Washington and im-
mersed himself in the stimulating chaos of the early New Deal.
In an administration which was innovative and experimental by
nature, college-trained young people were welcomed and accepted
as never before. Soon Tugwell successfully began to attract prom-
ising young men from Columbia. Among those drawn south to
Washington was his former student assistant, Roy Stryker. During
the summer of 1934, Stryker found a job with the recently created
Agricultural Adjustment Administration. Because it was a tem-
porary post, merely for the summer, Alice and their daughter
Phyllis remained in New York while Stryker moved in with Tugwell.[22] Since Tugwell's wife and children were in Europe, he was
pleased to have Stryker's company. The two got along well, in their
usual prickly way, and as the summer wore on there was even a
certain amount of communication between them.

Stryker's job was in the Information Division of the AAA, the
logical place for him since he had already developed a reputation
as a specialist in the use of illustrations. He helped write and
illustrate materials for the AAA under the direction of Milton
Eisenhower. His position gave him access to the picture file maintained at that time by the extension service of the Department
of Agriculture.[23] As the summer progressed, Stryker became more
and more aware of the wealth of visual information that lay in the
photographs, unfortunately unavailable to the average person.

One evening, late in the summer, he carefully formulated his
ideas and approached Tugwell. "You know, Rex, all those pictures

are just sitting down there going to waste. Why don't we do a
picture book on agriculture?" Tugwell quickly saw the direction
of Stryker's mind and grasped the possibilities. "It's a good idea,"
he said, "and you could go even further and make it a picture
source book on agriculture."[24] Tugwell envisioned careful use of
photographs to illustrate certain outstanding facts concerning
American farming so that the book could be a source book for
the historian or economist needing visual information, as well as
simply a picture book. There was, after all, an inherent value in
pictures as historical sources. Stryker liked Tugwell's ideas and,
with the senior officer's approval, began to devote some time to
planning a rough outline of the book. Once again Roy had an
idea and a project to work on. He was a happy man.

For the next year, the picture book on agriculture occupied
Stryker's spare time. In September, 1934, he returned to Columbia
University to resume his regular teaching duties, but the book
project was not allowed to die. That fall he worked with his old
friend Professor Harry Carman of the history department, completing and polishing the outline for the book.[25] The next spring
a grant was secured from the newly created National Youth Administration to finance some student aid. Now he could even
afford to hire some help. Stryker's initial idea had by now expanded. He was no longer planning to use only the files of the Department of Agriculture. Every magazine that appeared on the news-
stands was carefully searched for pictures that might be useful.
Even the library at Columbia was combed. Whenever he saw something that he thought might be included, a note went into his
pocket on a three by five card. By early spring he had amassed
an impressive collection—of three by five cards.[26]

The pictures that Stryker was compiling would be usable only
if they could be copied and reduced, or enlarged to a standard
size. Of course a photographer would have to do this. Stryker sent
word around the campus that a student familiar with cameras
was needed. The search turned up Arthur Rothstein, who had
taken the sophomore "Contemporary Civilization" course under
Stryker and had found the class stimulating and thought provok-
ing. Now in his senior year, Rothstein was planning to continue
his education in the sciences. He was considering medical school
but graduate work in chemistry was also attractive. In addition
to his interest in the sciences, there was photography. Rothstein
loved to take pictures. He loved cameras. Throughout college he
had spent a great deal of time using them. He had helped with the
production of the college yearbook; he had organized a camera

club; he had entered prints in the salon contests around New York—and won.[27] At the university it was generally understood that when matters concerning photography were under consideration, Arthur Rothstein would not be far away.

Stryker offered Rothstein the part-time job of copying the pictures that he was finding. Arthur happily agreed to work on the project, although the copy work was hardly challenging. He was feeling the pinch of the depression and the money would be welcomed. More important he welcomed the chance to work with his former teacher.[28] Throughout the spring of 1935, Stryker and his young assistant toiled away at the monumental project. Thousands of pictures passed through their hands and were copied, but when it was all over, they had no book. Perhaps Stryker had never gotten the project clearly enough in mind. Perhaps if there had been more time, a book would have emerged (for the collection was a valuable and well-selected record), but there was no more time. Stryker's attention was soon diverted and the project collapsed. Nevertheless the time had not been wasted, for the work on the book had been a learning experience.

That summer Stryker went down to Washington again: this time Tugwell had a new job for him. The Resettlement Administration had recently been formed, and Tugwell, as director of the agency, wanted someone who knew how to use pictures, both as a record of the project's activities and as a method of gaining national acceptance of the new programs. It promised to be a difficult, perhaps even a controversial job, but it gave Stryker a chance to work with pictures on a full-time basis. With Tugwell in charge of the program, Stryker could be sure of administrative protection and a certain degree of freedom. All things considered, it was an attractive opportunity.

The Resettlement Administration was a catchall organization, designed primarily to compensate for some important miscalculations in the older Agricultural Adjustment Act. The AAA had worked well enough for the larger, better-established farmer. It had limited his crops, to be sure, but it had also guaranteed a fair price for the smaller production. For the first time, the man who owned a good farm could calculate his income with reasonable accuracy at the beginning of the season. For the well-established farmer, this meant stability. For the tenant farmer or the renter, however, government programs of crop reduction too often meant displacement.

The problem had been foreseen. During the debate on the Triple A in 1933, Senator George Norris of Nebraska had raised the

28

Sign at a primitive
service station, 1935.
Ben Shahn.

Destitute family, Ozark
Mountains, Arkansas,
1935. Ben Shahn.
Library of Congress

possibility that the new program might throw people off the land. At that time Secretary of Agriculture Henry Wallace had been quick to reassure him that all payments for crop reduction would be divided between landowner and tenant. It seemed like the simple solution but unfortunately it was forgotten. No provision for dividing payments was written into the final AAA bill, and it became virtually impossible for most tenant farmers to collect any money for crops that were not being raised.[29] Landowners simply could not afford to leave land in production when they were being offered payment to let it lie fallow; so tens of thousands of tenants and sharecroppers were told to leave the land they had been farming.

In the South and Southwest, where as many as 75 percent of the people were tenants, the displacement was staggering.[30] The "Arkies" and "Okies" with their wretched cars and miserable families became a common sight along roadsides. John Steinbeck, in his classic *Grapes of Wrath,* caught the devastating effects of poverty and wandering on a rural family heading West in search of something better. Often, after selling everything and making the terrible hegira to California, the family found that their trip had been in vain. The labor market in the Far West was highly seasonal and easily saturated. When the crops were ready for harvest, cheap labor was needed; otherwise outsiders were unwelcome. State troopers were ever ready to break up encampments of emigrants and keep them moving. There was no rest and little work. For those who somehow managed to stay behind, clinging to worn-out land or working by the hour, the situation was often almost as bad. Living conditions on poor farms in the South have never been commodious, and in the mid-1930s they were a national disgrace.

Because the Agricultural Adjustment Act was not proving effective against the problems of the poorest one-third of American farmers and was, in many cases, worsening their lot, the Resettlement Administration was created. On April 30, 1935, President Roosevelt signed Executive Order 7027 which brought the new agency to life.[31] It was typical of the early experimental period of the New Deal, a hodgepodge of old programs that nobody wanted to administer, along with some very interesting new ideas. Because it was the creation of an executive order, the RA existed outside of the Department of Agriculture in a sort of bureaucratic twilight zone, without legal sanction or civil service status. Tugwell's own position was unusual. He became chief of the new agency yet retained his position as assistant secretary of agricul-

Heading toward Los
Angeles, California, 1937.
Dorothea Lange.

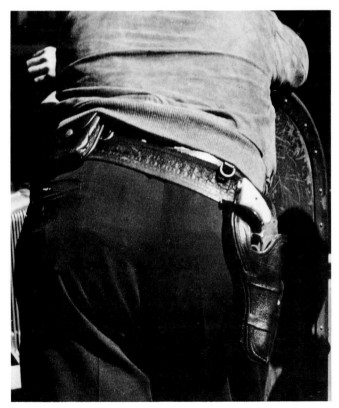

Deputy during strike,
Morgantown, West Virginia, 1935. Ben Shahn.

ture. Clearly he was becoming one of the really powerful young
men in Washington.

The President's order creating the Resettlement Administration
outlined three major areas of concern. There was to be a program
of low-interest loans to poor farmers who were burdened with
marginal or inadequate land. The object would be to help them
move to better farms and achieve landownership. There were to
be large projects in the areas of soil rebuilding and conservation.
The RA was empowered to buy large tracts of ruined land and
restore them to productivity. Forestation, curbing of stream pollution, programs to end flooding and erosion—all were to be within
its interests. Finally, there were a number of programs that came
under the general heading of resettlement.[32] Here were some
of the best and also some of the weakest aspects of the agency.

At its worst, Resettlement included the Subsistence Housing
program, an agency that Tugwell inherited from Harold Ickes at
the Department of the Interior. Subsistence Housing had been the
brainchild of Eleanor Roosevelt. It was supposed to move workers
and their families from the cities, where they were not needed,
to neat rural villages, where they were supposed to support themselves with home garden plots and part-time work. Because the
orderly mind of Ickes had boggled at the prospect of sending city
families into the country, he had not given the program his support.[33] Tugwell was not enthusiastic, either.[34] Eventually the program was absorbed into the vastly more practical Greenbelt Towns
project. Under this program the government built and operated
several successful suburban towns, near enough to large cities
so that commuting was practical.[35]

During the years of its existence, the Resettlement Administration set up several experimental communal farms for rural families
that had suffered displacement. These were highly controversial
because of their collectivistic nature. For many families they
represented a stopping-off point where a few years could be spent
while money was saved for a later new start on the land, but to
many outsiders the collective farms would always be "communis-
tic."[36] In addition to the communal farms, the RA sponsored
several more conventional rural communities. Farmers who
showed promise were allowed to buy farms in a specified area,
where land fertility was high and markets accessible. The government helped with loans and supervision.[37] Finally, the agency
sponsored camps for migrant farm laborers. Clean facilities and
low rents were made available to those who were forced to "follow
the crops."[38]

CCC boys at work on USDA Agricultural Research Center, Beltsville, Maryland, 1935. Carl Mydans. *Library of Congress*

Mountaineers "spelling" themselves in front of store, Pikesville, Tennessee. Carl Mydans. *Library of Congress*

These, in brief, were the programs that Tugwell had been asked to administer. All of them would not be popular. Tugwell understood this and so created an Information Division that was charged with the task of presenting the agency's positive programs and accomplishments to the country. It was within this division that Stryker was to function. As chief of the historical section of the Information Division of the Resettlement Administration, Stryker's name appeared far down on the organizational charts. Yet such charts can be and often are misleading. Because of his friendship with Tugwell, Stryker would be able to approach the top man when administrative problems arose.

Stryker was enthusiastic about his involvement with the Resettlement Administration, yet there were still hurdles. Shortly after his arrival in Washington in the summer of 1935, his health broke. His eyes began to trouble him again and a series of infections kept him miserable for weeks. He was edgy and terribly nervous about his job. At the end of the first month, he was thinking seriously about returning to teaching. Tugwell, as usual, adopted the tough approach which always seemed to work so well on Roy:

> You see, originally, I went down to start with Farm Security [Resettlement Administration] and then I had to come back because my eye was causing me a lot of trouble. I went to Tugwell and said, "Rex, look I think I ought to drop out of this." He looked at me—that was the wonderful thing about Rex—he was curt and sharp to me, but underneath it all, I realized how much it meant—and he said, "Now, look, you cut out that stuff and go someplace and do a little thinking—you don't have to use your eyes to think, do you? Don't give me any of that stuff about quitting."[39]

It never failed. Tugwell knew that the one thing Stryker could not do was to back away from a challenge. Stryker decided to remain in Washington. Shortly afterward his eyes began to improve and a series of trips to the dentist cleared up the infections. His disposition softened and he began to settle into serious work with pictures. The evolution of the finest collection of American documentary photographs ever assembled could begin.

The young man who had come as a country boy to conquer New York City had finally found his niche. In a very real sense, all of his experiences leading up to this point had served to create the unique blend that made him perfectly suited to his task. Those early years in Montrose and the Uncompaghre Valley had given him a love of the land and a love of agriculture that he would never lose. His family's respect for learning and his own bookish-

Gossip at the fair,
Vermont. Carl Mydans.

American Countryside.
Carl Mydans.

tion Division and the control of Roy Stryker.[8] It seems clear that Tugwell's long acquaintance with Stryker and their warm friendship had provided the necessary margin of trust. Stryker had said that the agency should have a unified photographic service. Very well, Stryker would be the obvious choice to run it.

The order from Tugwell accomplished several things. It convinced Roy that he was genuinely needed in Washington and that his ideas would carry some influence. Until this time his commitment to the Resettlement Administration had been only partial. He had been interested in the experiments going on in Washington but had not really felt a part of things. His correspondence with faculty members at Columbia University indicated that he had not given up the idea of returning to teaching in the fall.[9] Now, however, all thoughts of turning back were put away. The order gave Stryker full responsibility for the development of photographic representation of the work of the RA. This meant that he could begin to make meaningful decisions in both the areas of technique and esthetics.

In the early days, many of the technical decisions were made by Arthur Rothstein. His interest in cameras and other photographic hardware amounted to almost a passion, and his knowledge of the mechanics of photography far surpassed Roy's. Arthur understood that the agency's reputation for fine photography could grow only on a solid technical base. Without a good darkroom and skilled technicians, the greatest pictures in the world would be worthless.[10] In the fall of 1935, the facilities available for darkroom work were little short of appalling. The Department of Agriculture had a darkroom that the historical section could use, if it wanted to, but the equipment was so out of date that it could handle nothing more modern than glass plate negatives.[11] This simply would not do, and it became Rothstein's responsibility to scout around for equipment and men. By the end of 1935, he had made a good beginning. The historical section had a fair, if somewhat basic, darkroom and good men to run it.

The order from Tugwell consolidating all photographic work under Stryker's direction also brought other advantages. In the reshuffling that followed, he gained two new photographers, both men from whom he could learn much. Carl Mydans and Walker Evans joined the historical section, bringing with them new ideas and new points of view. In different ways, each was an experienced photographer who could contribute much to Stryker's developing visual sense. They could help him clarify the goals of his agency.

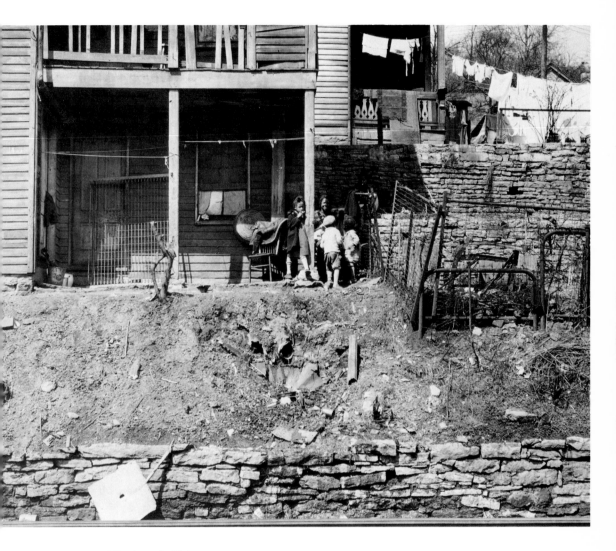

Cincinnati, Ohio.
Carl Mydans.

Carl Mydans came to government photography from a journalistic background. While in college in Boston, he had worked as a writer for the Boston *Globe* and the Boston *Herald*. After graduation he came to New York as a financial reporter for the *American Banker*, a Wall Street newspaper. During the years in which he was working in the Wall Street area, Mydans began to use the camera. It has been suggested that the camera provided him with a pleasant escape from the routine of financial reporting.[12] Whatever his reasons, Mydans soon had a 35mm camera and was enthusiastically prowling the streets of New York City in search of pictures. He was particularly interested in the everyday lives of people. With his trained reporter's eye, Mydans quickly developed a style of his own that fitted his people-oriented approach. With his small cameras, he was able to achieve pictures that were striking yet intimate.

Eventually people in New York began to notice the work Mydans was doing, but the magazines and newspapers had little use for his style. Work done with a 35mm was not being taken seriously in those days. Editors considered it grainy and unsharp and photographers considered the tiny cameras toys. Few people could see the potential in the small cameras. For Mydans the break finally came when a friend on the staff of *Time* heard of an opening in the Suburban Resettlement Administration in Washington.[13] Mydans was interviewed for the job. In Washington he found people who were far more receptive to new ideas and miniature camera techniques than the New York editors had been. A brilliant young editor named Robert Thorpe had recently been hired by the agency to do a book on the activities of Suburban Resettlement. Thorpe and Mydans worked for several months on the book.[14] Their ideas were graphic and ahead of their time. It turned out to be quite a book, but it also turned out to be too expensive to print. Even so, Suburban Resettlement gained a reputation around Washington as the place where interesting work in graphics was taking place.

When the Resettlement Administration was created, Suburban Resettlement was one of the agencies transferred from the Department of the Interior to Tugwell's group. Later, when all photographic activities were combined under Stryker, Mydans joined the historical section. Stryker was aware of the high quality work that had been going on at Suburban Resettlement, and he was happy to have Mydans join his unit. He later recalled: "Carl came in with hundreds of feet of 35mm film. I had never seen anybody take so many pictures! We had to spread everything out on the

Butcher sign, Mississippi,
1936. Walker Evans.

Hale County, Alabama,
1935. Walker Evans.

floor of the office just to see what he had. It was wonderful!"[15] Mydans made a real contribution to the development of the historical section with his trained reporter's eye and his dynamic approach to people. Roy had seen plenty of 35mm film before because Arthur Rothstein had used it for both copying and field work, but Roy had never seen the full potential of 35mm as thoroughly explored as Mydans did it. Stryker and his men would never adopt 35mm or any other format exclusively. In fact, just about every conceivable camera and film size would be used, but Mydan's ability to use a small camera to capture fleeting attitudes and expressions assured that Stryker would never consider the small camera a toy.

Walker Evans was as different from the other photographers who made up the early historical section as it was possible for a man to be. Rothstein had done his early work on campus newspapers and yearbooks. He had competed in salon exhibitions and had developed an eye for the picture that could win prizes. Mydans had walked the streets of New York capturing on film fleeting moments that were meaningful. Evans' approach was unlike either of the others'. In his own deliberate, careful way, Walker Evans was an artist with a camera. He loved to take a large, awkward view camera and capture one picture that summed up the whole statement that he wanted to make in a kind of bitter, almost cynical beauty.

Evans was the product of a puritanical home in the Middle West. Although he left home in Missouri when he decided to attend college in Massachusetts and never again lived west of the Mississippi, the influence of his parents and their harsh New England background remained strong.[16] His photographic style developed the sort of merciless directness that one associates with Grant Wood's "American Gothic." After college, Evans spent some time in Paris where he came in contact with some of the best photography in Europe. He worked for a time under the French portraitist Nadar, and he saw the fine pictures that Eugene Atget had made of Paris around the turn of the century.[17] In the late 1920s he returned to the United States and began to build a reputation for himself. Hart Crane, the poet, featured his photographs in a book titled *The Bridge*.[18] The exclusive, beautifully printed magazine, *Hound and Horn*, also began to use his work.

In a way Evans was working in the tradition of Alfred Stieglitz. His pictures were carefully and respectfully done. He expected in return that they be used carefully and with respect. He did not take large numbers of photographs, but those he took were im-

Bridge and houses,
Easton, Pennsylvania,
1935. Walker Evans.
Library of Congress

Graveyard and steel mill,
Bethlehem, Pennsylvania,
1935. Walker Evans.
Library of Congress

mediately recognizable as his own. By 1933 he had developed
what would become a lifelong connection with the New York
Museum of Modern Art. At this point the work that he was doing
for the museum was not of long-range interest: he was merely
hired to photograph a large collection of African artifacts. Later,
however, the friendships formed at this stage would give rise to
better things. In 1938 Evans was given the first one-man show that
the museum had ever produced. Eventually his finest collection
of photographs would be published under the auspices of the
museum.[19]

Life was difficult in the early thirties for a rather socially in-
hibited young photographer who fiercely insisted on taking himself and his work seriously. For a while Evans shared a studio
on Bethune Street in the upper Greenwich Village area of New
York with two other equally hard-up young men. Lou Block, one
of those who shared the Bethune Street studio, was a painter and
would later play a key role in the Federal Arts Project. The third
occupant was the painter Ben Shahn. During the early thirties,
the three men lived a tight, hand-to-mouth existence. Evans seldom talked about his work, and Block later would remember that
nobody ever knew whether Walker was eating or not. Somehow he
managed to get film and paper but food often had to be foregone.[20]

When the government began to use artists and photographers,
Evans decided to see if he could fit in. He began to do some part-
time work for the Department of the Interior, and while the assignments were not exactly to his taste, he needed the money
badly and stuck with it. In the summer of 1935, he heard of the
work that was just getting started in the Resettlement Administration. Evans talked to a friend of his, Ernestine Evans, a skilled
writer and editor who was at that time working in the Subsistence
Housing program. Miss Evans was impressed enough with the
photographs she saw to take the matter up with the Chief of Information, John Franklin Carter.[21] Soon a meeting was arranged
between Stryker and Walker Evans.

The two men hit it off immediately. Evans found Stryker to be
openminded if not very clear as to directions. Stryker, on the
other hand, was tremendously impressed with Evans' cool pro-
fessionalism. On October 9, 1935, Walker Evans joined the staff
of the historical section.[22] He had waited a long time to eat regularly and now he was ready to drive a hard bargain. The job description called him "Senior Information Specialist," and his salary
was considerably higher than either Rothstein's or Mydans'. Obviously at this point Stryker was convinced that Evans was worth

Ferry and wharf goods,
Vicksburg, Mississippi,
1936. Walker Evans.

the price. A careful search of the photofiles of the project now
in the Library of Congress bears out this initial judgment. Evans
was a magnificent photographer. Entering the project as he did,
in the early formative months, he helped to set a standard of excellence that affected almost all of the people who joined the section later. His work was consistently of the very highest technical
quality and it usually carried an unmistakable message. Unfortunately, Evans was neither prolific nor particularly cooperative.
In a government agency, these traits could lead to trouble. In the
fall of 1935, however, there was no friction, only long walks and
probing conversations as Evans tried to articulate his feelings
and Stryker tried to understand.

For Walker Evans, the deepest, indeed the only responsibility of
the artist was to his subject matter. Whether the subject was a person or a house or a chair, if it was meaningful to the artist he
owed it his total concentration. Evans lived for the creative act.
The agency that hired him was unimportant. The plans they might
have for the photographs were unimportant. The really important
things were the act of finding and securing the picture and the
picture itself. Roy might not agree with Evans' approach to photography, but he could not help admiring its singleminded totality of
commitment to excellence.[23]

While Evans was drumming away at the need for perfection in
the agency, his old friend Ben Shahn was showing Stryker other
valuable approaches to pictures. Shahn was not even a photographer in the usual sense of the word and was not officially employed by the historical section, yet he played an important role
in clarifying the ways that the historical section could use photographs. Shahn was a painter, lithographer, and an expert in murals. In earlier days he had worked with Diego Rivera.[24] He was
hired in the fall of 1935 by the Special Skills Division of the Resettlement Administration.[25] Special Skills was the division concerned with the fine arts, painting, posters, and even interior
decoration of RA offices. Shahn had been recommended to the
director of Special Skills by the same young woman who had
helped Walker Evans get his job. Ernestine Evans knew talent
when she saw it. She also knew which people to talk to, and Shahn
was hired.

As a painter and designer for Special Skills, Shahn was encouraged to find out as much about the total program of the RA as he
could. Very shortly after joining the agency he was sent out into
the field on an extended tour of the South and Southwest. For
three months Shahn drove about the country absorbing as much

Rehabilitation client, Boone County, Arkansas, 1935.
Ben Shahn. *Library of Congress*

Priest at Pointe a la
Hache, Louisiana, 1935.
Ben Shahn. *Library of
Congress*

as he could. As an aid to his memory, he took hundreds of pictures with a Leica 35mm camera.[26] These pictures were originally intended as raw material for murals and posters, and many were later used for that purpose. The pictures were so good, however, that Roy asked if the final prints could be placed in the file of the historical section. Shahn would still have access to the pictures when he needed them, but the pictures could also stand on their own as fine photographs.

Shahn had an ability few could match for capturing the torture in the body of a farm wife, old before her time, or the terror in the eyes of a drought-scarred child. As an established artist, Shahn could also speak with authority on the subject of visuals. Stryker looked at his pictures and listened to his ideas, and learned. Unlike most of the painters of his day, Shahn did not shun the word "propaganda." He used the term in a neutral sense, connoting a visual teaching device. He accepted and approved the teaching role that pictures were being asked to play in the Resettlement Administration. His art had always had a point of view. He had always taken a position. In fact, some of his earliest and best-known work had been in defense of Sacco and Vanzetti, the two philosophical anarchists whose deaths had come to symbolize the harshest civil rights repression of the 1920s.[27] Now the job was to teach Americans about farm problems. To do this Shahn understood that the best possible pictures would be needed.

In those early days, when Stryker was still groping for directions, talk, critique, endless sessions of looking at pictures, and personal growth were the order of the day. Shahn enjoyed these sessions and contributed to them as often as he could. Once he became involved in a discussion concerning a picture of eroded soil. Stryker liked the photograph. It was nice and sharp and it really did show what water could do to the land. Shahn was not so sure about the picture. "Look, Roy," he said, "You're not going to move anybody with this eroded soil—but the effect this eroded soil has on a kid who looks starved, this is going to move people. You just can't move anybody with this kind of photograph."[28] In dozens of exchanges of this sort, the chief and his photographers learned from one another and developed their overall approach to photography.

It was also during the first fall that Roy saw Dorothea Lange's pictures. The photographer from California had been deeply involved in the fight against the depression for several years. Her initial photographic experience had been fairly conventional; she had been running a portrait studio in Berkeley, taking nice, safe

Waiting outside rural
relief station, Urbana,
Ohio, 1938. Ben Shahn.
Library of Congress

pictures of nice, safe people. When economic disaster struck the country, however, and the sad column of jalopies began to roll into California, Dorothea Lange knew that somehow she had to be a part of the fight to win better conditions for the poor. In 1933 she had made "White Angel Bread Line," a picture that caught the eye of photographer Willard Van Dyke.[29] Van Dyke featured the photograph prominently in an exhibition that he was sponsoring, and soon Lange had a job. The picture was seen by a young professor of economics at the University of California, Paul Schuster Taylor. Taylor realized that Lange had hit upon a direct and honest photographic style that could be used effectively in the economic battle, and he immediately enlisted her. Taylor and Lange worked together on several articles and projects. *Survey Graphic* featured their work several times, and in 1935 they collaborated on a report for the California State Relief Administration.[30] The report went to Washington, where it crossed the desk of Rexford Tugwell and eventually came to Stryker's attention.

Ben Shahn was present when Lange's work was brought into the office. He never forgot its impact. "Dorothea's work was sent in or brought in by somebody and this was a revelation, what this woman was doing."[31] Lange had very strong feelings about social injustice and her feelings came through clearly in her photographs. There were few ambiguities here, just pictures that hammered away at the senses with bludgeonlike impact. The viewer was forced to look upon human misery directly, without palliatives, yet the photographs were also beautiful, dignified, and sympathetic. Lange was quickly contacted and added to the payroll, and Stryker gained new lessons and ideas from her pictures. Because she did not come to Washington until the next spring, Lange did not take part in those early, highly important discussions and critiques. Her work was done separately in the early days and primarily on the West Coast. Even so, Lange's pictures spoke for her and had a tremendous influence on the formative period of the historical section.

By the end of 1935, Roy had an agency established. He had four good photographers, Rothstein, Mydans, Evans, and Lange. He had the friendly advice and guidance of Ben Shahn when he needed it. The technical problems of establishing the darkroom and beginning the picture file were beginning to work themselves out. Most important, some significant photographic corners had been turned, and Stryker was beginning to get a fairly clear idea of the direction that his section should take. After hundreds of cups of coffee had been consumed and hundreds of photographs looked at,

Filipinos working in lettuce field, Salinas, California, 1935. Dorothea Lange.

Migratory farm laborer on the Pacific Coast, California, 1936. Dorothea Lange. *Library of Congress*

discussed, and mulled over, he knew that his people could accomplish a significant document of the American way of life in the 1930s. There would be no more copying of office memos. Writing in 1939 one expert in the field of government publicity outlined the objects that Stryker had worked out for his agency:

> The basic assumption shared by the Administration and the Section Chief, was that a government agency should consider its function to be much broader than the mere performance of duties commanded by the job assigned. It should, in fact, consider its role against the background of American life as a whole and should recognize its role in the total scheme of social processes. In picture taking, this meant that the Resettlement Administration photographers should first record . . . the performance of the agency's primary job, which was to administer rural relief. . . . The second part of the photographer's job would be to record and report the milieu in which the agency performed its primary function. As a result, the photographers took pictures of nearly any subject that was significant as a document of American culture.[32]

In recent years, it has become common to see Roy Stryker given complete credit for the development and direction of the historical section. In a sense, of course, such credit is well placed, for he did recognize the talent that people possessed and he had a fine instinct for hiring the very best. On the other hand, it must be emphasized that in the early days, Stryker too was learning. The later directions that the historical section took can only be fully understood when one knows the personalities that made up the first historical section "team." Each man and woman had something to contribute. Each brought his own personality and his own approach to pictures. The combination of these elements laid the foundation for the tremendous creative outpouring of the next several years.

IV

Stryker and
the Photographers:
The Early Years

By the end of 1935, Roy Stryker and the small group of photographers that he had assembled were well on their way to a clear understanding of their photographic goals. At the same time, Stryker was beginning to understand his own job better. It was becoming clear that he would have to be prepared to function on several levels. At times he would have to put on his armor and become the defender of his agency; at other times he would have to function as the disciplinarian. At all times he must act as director, teacher, and sympathetic listener to the photographers. Because he was dealing with persons of great talent and considerable ego, it was well that Stryker decided very early to take no photographs himself. In this way he was left completely free to guide and motivate without becoming caught up in either the mechanics of photography or any specific stylistic approach.

Stryker's role as director was sometimes conditioned by political or bureaucratic changes outside his control. A change in the political climate or a change in the organization of the agency could bring great adjustments. A year during which Congress was willing to appropriate large sums of money might be more pleasant than one in which it suffered a fit of parsimony. A sympathetic Chief of the Information Division could make life easier for Stryker, while an unsympathetic man could put the very existence of his unit in jeopardy. In 1937 the entire agency went through a major change when the autonomous Resettlement Administration was absorbed into the huge and impersonal United States Department of Agriculture. At this point the name was changed to the Farm Security Administration and, more important from Stryker's point of view, Rexford Tugwell resigned as administrator.[1] After

1937 there would be fewer friendly faces and willing ears in the front office when Stryker wanted to discuss a problem.

All of these factors set the limits within which Stryker had to work, yet they could not be allowed to dominate his thinking. It was especially important that the photographers in the field be insulated from petty institutional problems. Dorothea Lange once described Stryker as a "colossal watchdog for his people."[2] It was a description that he would have liked if he had known about it, for he often thought of himself in the same way. In the early days, Ben Shahn wondered whether Roy was really accomplishing anything or was "just another bureaucrat." "But I soon realized that without Roy this thing would have died. He was the one who was constantly up on the hill and constantly manipulating and so forth —making it possible for us to go out into the field, to be protected by him—and for this I was grateful."[3]

In dealing with the photographers, Stryker developed an individualized approach, tailoring his instructions to the needs of each person. His letters to Arthur Rothstein, for example, were quite different from his letters to Dorothea Lange. Stryker seemed to know intuitively how to draw the maximum effort from each person. This is, of course, the mark of a great teacher, and throughout his career in the development of documentary photography, he remained primarily a great teacher.

When a photographer of the historical section prepared to go into the field to investigate a specific problem or group of problems, he was expected to make proper preparations. Proper cameras, film, and the like were taken for granted, but mental preparation was Stryker's business. Before a photographer went into a region, he was given all the information that Stryker could muster concerning the area, its people, its economy, and even its politics and social mores. Often the photographer would have a list of specific pictures to look out for. Such lists later became elaborate "shooting scripts." In addition to these, there might be informal sessions with people in Washington who knew the region well. There would be long talks with Stryker and there would often be books to read. Stryker loved to force his people to think a problem through in a new way. He was convinced that if a sensitive photographer entered a region with a deep understanding of the forces at work in the area, his photographs would mirror both his understanding and his compassion.

No story better illustrates Stryker's function as a director of photographers than Carl Mydans' memory of his own first encounter with Stryker, the educator. ". . . my assignment was to go

Children of rehabilitation clients, Yakima, Washington, 1936. Arthur Rothstein. *Library of Congress*

Gee's Bend, Alabama, 1937. Arthur Rothstein.

South and 'do cotton.' I put my camera together and drew my
film . . . and I came in to tell Roy Stryker that I was on my way.
He greeted me goodby and wished me luck and then he looked
at me and said, 'By the way, what do you know about cotton?' I
stopped and said, 'Not very much.'"

The Columbia economics teacher asked a few more probing
questions. Mydans answered as best he could, with a growing
awareness that he didn't really have the answers. Finally Stryker
said, "Sit down. What you indicate is that you know *nothing* about
cotton!" "He called in his secretary and said, 'Cancel Carl's transportation. He's going to stay here with me for a while.' And we
sat down and we talked almost all day about cotton. We went to
lunch and we went to dinner, and we talked well into the night.
He talked about cotton as an agricultural product, cotton as a
commercial product, the history of cotton in the South, what
cotton did to the history of the U.S.A. and how it affected areas
outside the U.S.A. By the end of that evening, I was ready to go off
and photograph cotton!"[4]

In situations like this, Stryker was at his best. He had an ency-
clopedic knowledge of the socioeconomic forces at work in the
various regions of the United States, and he loved to teach from
this basis. Bolstered by a healthy dose of such enthusiastic informal scholarship, a photographer's work was certain to show the
impact of the new information. This insistence that photographers
in the field know exactly what it was they were photographing
and how it related to the overall regional socioeconomic picture
was one of the primary factors that made the pictures taken by the
historical section different from other photographs being taken
at the time.

Stryker wanted his people to have a complete grasp of the social
scene they were documenting. If they could be informed best by
informal sessions, that was fine, but he soon discovered a need for
compact sources of specific information that people could carry
along on their trips. Each historical section photographer was
told to buy a copy of J. Russell Smith's socioeconomic geography
book, *North America*. Smith was a geographer who had taught for
years at Columbia University. Stryker had known him there and
had developed a great respect for his thorough regional investi-
gations. *North America* covered the entire continent, region by
region. If a photographer needed information on a specific point,
such as the importance of the sugar beet industry in Michigan, he
had only to consult Smith's book and the material was there. If
he needed to gain a better understanding of what had gone wrong

Pennsylvania steel town.
Walker Evans.

with the mining industry in West Virginia, he would find a short
but clear discussion of the problem.[5] It was not a small book nor
was it the sort of thing that one would read from cover to cover,
but it was a fine, handy source book, and it gave the photographers much needed direction when they were in unfamiliar situations. In addition to *North America,* most of the photographers
carried maps, United States Department of Agriculture pamphlets,
and anything else that might give some insight into the regions
that they were dealing with.[6]

During the first two years of the historical section's existence,
the agency was quite problem oriented. The photographers felt
the immediacy of the nation's rural troubles and the need for
pictures to make these problems clear to the rest of the country.
Many of the saddest, starkest, most difficult pictures to view were
made during this time. The years 1935 to 1937 were terribly hard
for small farmers and tenant farmers. It took time for federal aid
programs to have an impact. By 1937 and thereafter, there would
be positive sides of the story to tell, stories of families rescued
and fine new farms established, but at the beginning there were
only problems. Stryker's main interest lay in putting into the field
photographers who understood the problems and possessed the
sensitivity to portray them for the nation. To do this successfully,
he had to deal with each photographer in a way that would bring
about the best possible production.

Walker Evans was a photographer who required special handling. In the early days he was the designated senior photographer.
Stryker was tremendously impressed with the stark simplicity and
selectivity of his approach. Unlike Ben Shahn, however, Evans never quite saw the value of Stryker's role. He never felt that Stryker
could teach him anything; thus Stryker was forced to let him
pretty much alone, to find his own way. Evans' way was to disap-
pear for months at a time, keep no clear records of where he had
been or was going, and finally to reappear with a small number of
the finest photographs ever taken. For two years Stryker allowed
Evans to set his own pace and the results certainly justified his
patience. No one ever took better photographs than Walker Evans.
On the other hand, Evans' approach to photography made life
difficult in a government bureaucracy. The budget bureau wanted
to know where Stryker's senior photographer was, why he didn't
turn in the travel forms that they regarded as so important, and
why he didn't take more pictures? (Budget people count things.
They do not look at them or assess their esthetic value.) Often
Stryker's patience wore thin; yet those beautiful pictures contin-

Negro house, Tupelo,
Mississippi, 1936.
Walker Evans.

Shop front, Vicksburg,
Mississippi, 1936.
Walker Evans.

ued to come in from time to time; and Evans stayed on the payroll.

As long as he remained with the historical section, Walker Evans was given as much freedom as possible. He was seldom asked to take the sort of dull, routine "progress pictures" that all of the other photographers had to do, and hated. He was seldom sent out to the experimental farms or planned communities to stand the local director and his assistant, smiling, up against an unfinished wall and photograph them. On occasion a list of towns to visit along with some general subjects would be sent out, but that was about all. For example, during the early part of the summer of 1936, Evans was on an extended trip through the South when a letter arrived at his hotel in Vicksburg, Mississippi. The tone of the letter was conciliatory:

> Dear Walker,
> We had a little consultation here yesterday . . . and this is the results of our efforts. . . . Of course, we concede your right to modify, since you are on the ground and may see good reasons why you should go one place instead of another; but in general I do think it [the following set of instructions] will give you the opportunity to photograph the type of things which we want most.

Stryker went on to suggest several towns that he wanted Evans to visit and photograph. One of these was Birmingham, Alabama: "I would suggest that you spend several days around Birmingham. There is no need to go into detail as to what you will do there. I am sure that you will have a grand time with your eye for industrial landscapes. Wire us as soon as you get there so we can reach you . . . ."[7]

The route of the proposed trip lay through Georgia, northern Florida, and South Carolina. There were several Resettlement Administration projects in that area of which Stryker needed photographs. He was, however, obviously reluctant to use Evans for this sort of "project work." "This is one of the emergency jobs that I hate to bother you with, but it must be done," Stryker remarked to Evans after asking him to photograph an RA project near Tupelo, Mississippi.[8] Finally, near the end of the long letter, Stryker made reference to the fact that Evans was not taking a large number of pictures. Clearly Evans' irregular working methods and his low rate of production were beginning to cause problems for Stryker: "I realize this is a nice big order, but remember you've got to deliver or I am going to catch the devil."[9]

A few weeks later a second letter caught up with Evans at St. Marys, Georgia, near the Florida border. The tone was still careful; Stryker valued Evans' services and wanted to keep him with the historical section as long as he could. Nevertheless there was a

Roadside sandwich shop, Ponchatoula, Louisiana,
1936. Walker Evans.

Negro houses, Atlanta,
Georgia, 1936. Walker
Evans.

real problem developing with the budget bureau. Evans was simply not taking enough pictures to keep the upstairs bureaucrats happy. Stryker wrote that he needed more pictures and better cooperation. "Your monthly expenditures look pretty large and unless I can lay down lots of pictures with your name on them each month, I am afraid I am going to be in for some difficulty. . . . After all, the Resettlement Administration is putting out to you each month a pretty nice sum of money and they have a right to expect certain returns. Their ideas differ somewhat from yours perhaps, but the way for you to get the opportunity of doing the thing you want is to satisfy them."[10]

In view of the problems developing, both men were probably relieved when Evans was asked by *Fortune* to see if he could get a leave of absence from his government job for a couple of months. *Fortune* wanted him to collaborate with his friend James Agee in a photographic and textual study of southern sharecroppers. The idea was for the two men to actually live with several sharecropper families and to experience fully their lives and miseries. It was a new approach to reform literature and the possibilities excited Agee and Evans. With Stryker's blessing, the leave of absence for Walker was arranged. It was to begin on July 16, 1936, and last for two months.[11] If necessary the leave could be extended. During this time, Evans would be paid by *Fortune.*

The magazine assignment turned out to be a creative high point for both James Agee and Walker Evans. To the immense disgust of the editors of *Fortune,* the two men did not produce a short article on sharecropping. Instead their work bloomed and developed into a full-sized book, and quite a book it was! *Let Us Now Praise Famous Men* was too much for any magazine. It was too rich in photographs and imagery. It was too committed in ideology. It was too deeply felt. The cumulative effect was so powerful that editor after editor rejected the book. They could not risk money publishing a book that was sure to be misunderstood by many people. As a result, *Let Us Now Praise Famous Men* was not brought out until 1941.[12] Tragically, by that time the sense of immediacy had been lost. The book became a classic but only a historical one. Had it been published in 1936, it could have been a classic in reform literature, a classic of reform propaganda in the great tradition of Riis and Hine.

There is irony in the relationship between Stryker and Evans. Both men wanted to use photographs to tell the country about rural problems. Both men wanted to help bring new approaches and depths of understanding to the medium of photography. Even

64

"Bud" Fields family,
Alabama, 1936. Walker
Evans.

so, when they attempted to work together, neither was as effective as he might have been. Evans became truculent and hard to work with; Stryker became more and more assertive of his own prerogatives as section chief. It was only outside the strictures of the government job that Evans could really reach his fullest potential. Yet the months of travel in the South at government expense, the talks with Stryker, the period of time without money worries that the Resettlement Administration had provided all helped him to develop his photographic eye and his personal awareness to the degree that could result in *Let Us Now Praise Famous Men.*

By the summer of 1937, Evans would leave the Resettlement Administration to engage in independent work. As an administrator Stryker could hardly have been sorry to see him go. Yet as a lover of fine photographs, Stryker must have known what a loss the historical section had sustained. Perhaps Dorothea Lange summed up the sort of man that Walker Evans was better than anyone else. Not long before her death, she was asked by a friend if Evans was a problem child. "A problem child? I don't know whether he is a problem child to himself. But when anyone asks me what do I know about someone who is an artist, I can only answer, 'Please look at his work. . . .' There is a bitterness. . . . There is an edge, a bitter edge to Walker—that I sense—and it is pleasurable to me. I like that bitter edge."

Lange went on to recall Evans' honesty and his straightforward approach to life. Then she turned her attention to the problems that had developed between Walker and Roy.

> Now on Farm Security. The first, before I met him [Evans] I heard Roy complaining—Walker had been out in the South for six weeks and they'd never heard from him. They didn't know where he was. "We haven't gotten a single thing! He's been out for six weeks, and when he comes back to the office I'm going to tell him. . . ." But Walker was like that. He would be completely oblivious to the fact that this was an office struggling to justify its existence. He just took his paychecks and disappeared. But where was he? He was down with Agee and the result was *Let Us Now Praise Famous Men,* you see? Walker is a small producer. He's not a big producer . . . [but] I think he is a good American photographer, by Jove I do.[13]

As a director Roy could not have been completely happy with his handling of Walker Evans. Among the many talented people who would at one time or another work for the historical section, the Stryker-Evans relationship was one of the least successful. Could it have been different if Evans had come into the agency at a later time, when Stryker was more sure of his own leadership? Undoubtedly Stryker asked himself that question many

Negro church, South
Carolina, 1936. Walker
Evans.

times, yet there was no answer. Evans was a loner, an egotist who simply had to find his own way. For a while his path crossed that of the historical section. When he was gone, he left it enriched.

In direct contrast to the cool detachment of Walker Evans, Dorothea Lange was a person who needed to know that her work was finding favor. Stryker's approach to her and her work always had to take into consideration the fact that she genuinely valued his approval and wanted to know that her pictures were being used. In one instance, when a member of the Information Division, who was not directly connected with the historical section, criticized some of her pictures, Dorothea wrote to Roy: "I don't care at all about this irascible gentleman down the hall . . . , or what he thinks. But I do care if I have angered you and I do care to hold your confidence in my actions."[14] In another case, when Roy had not had time to write any of his well-known rambling letters for several weeks, Dorothea wrote plaintively, "How about a letter to your little step-child?"[15]

Because she spent most of her time on the West Coast, Lange always felt a bit isolated, away from the creative mainstream in Washington. Because of this, Stryker was always careful to include in his letters to her the meaningful little pieces of news from Washington that would make her feel a part of the group. Often, when one of the other photographers was off on a major trip, he included their latest experiences and tribulations. If the political situation in Washington was changing, the news was mentioned and speculated upon. In one of his earliest letters to Dorothea, long before the two had actually met, he told her that her work had been recommended to Charles Wilson, author of *Backwoods America*. Wilson was working on a new book, tentatively titled *Roots of America*, and he had agreed that Lange's work was just what he needed for illustrations. "He will be very glad to give credit both to the Resettlement Administration and to the photographer. This book will have a very wide circulation as Funk and Wagnalls are using it as a premium book,"[16] Roy wrote. Even at this early stage, Roy knew the words that photographers loved to hear.

Stryker's directions to Dorothea were more specific than those he sent to Walker Evans, yet they were usually conversational in tone. Stryker respected Lange's ability and wanted her to have as much freedom as possible. In early 1936 she was preparing for her first major trip for the Resettlement Administration. The planned itinerary would take her into the agricultural areas of Southern California and over into Arizona and New Mexico. After

Arkansas mother in
California for new start,
with husband and eleven
children. A rural rehabil-
itation client, Tulare,
California, 1938.
Dorothea Lange.
Library of Congress

Refugee families near
Holtville, California, 1937.
Dorothea Lange.

writing his formal approval of the project, Stryker offered a few
friendly suggestions.

> Would you, in the next few days, take for us some good slum pictures
> in the San Francisco area. (Of course, no California city has slums,
> but I'll bet you can find them.) We need to vary the diet in some of
> our exhibits here by showing some western poverty instead of all
> south and east. . . . When you get to Los Angeles, I think it might be
> worthwhile to see if you can pick up some good slum pictures there
> also. Do not forget that we need some of the rural slum type of thing,
> as well as the urban. . . .
>
> As you are driving along through the agricultural areas and if you
> can do it without too much extra effort, would you take a few shots of
> various types of farm activities such as your picture showing the lettuce
> workers. I think Dr. Tugwell would be very appreciative of photographs
> of this sort to be used as illustrative material for some things which
> the Department of Agriculture is working on.[17]

Letters of this type were common. Stryker liked to explain why
a certain picture was needed at a given time. Of course if he was
in a rush, as he often was, extra information like this might be
left out of letters and simply discussed later when director and
photographer got together. In the case of Dorothea Lange, however, distance prevented frequent meetings and thus the letters
tended to be quite detailed.

Stryker also liked to know what his photographers were thinking and what sort of problems they were encountering. He encouraged them to write detailed accounts of their experiences in the
field. No one did this better than Lange. Like her camera, her pen
was a vigorous tool that reflected exactly how she felt. In one of
her earliest letters to Stryker, she described her feelings and im-
pressions to the director whom she had not met. "It's late and
I'm tired," she wrote. "Had a good day today but I'm done up—and
there are all those notes and explanations, essays on the social
scene in California is what they should be—still to be done."
Lange described her trip through driving rain in the agricultural
district around San Luis and her attempts to get pictures in the
bad weather. "Tried to work in the pea camps in heavy rain from
the back of the station wagon. I doubt that I got anything. Made
other mistakes too, which will be all too apparent to you." Finally,
Lange voiced a frustration that is familiar to every serious photographer: "I make the most mistakes on subject matter that I get
excited about and enthusiastic. In other words, the worse the
work, the richer the material was."[18]

In December, 1935, Dorothea Lange married Paul Taylor, the
California economist with whom she had been working so close-

"Migrant Mother,"
California, 1936.
Dorothea Lange.

71

ly.[19] The next spring Taylor had some work to do for the Department of Agriculture in Washington, and the two were able to come to the capital together. For the first time Stryker and Lange were able to meet and spend some time together. The two hit it off as well in person as they had on paper. There was time for talking, for discussing aims and ways pictures could be used. There was time for Lange to explore the growing file of photographs which the historical section was accumulating. In a letter to a friend on the staff of the *Nation* she described her enthusiasm over what she had found. "The files here in Washington are rich," she wrote. "I wish you could see them."[20]

Lange was impressed with the photographic files, but she was even more struck by a certain atmosphere of freedom that seemed to pervade the office of the historical section. On the surface the agency was certainly not impressive. It was disorganized, crammed into hot, uncomfortable quarters, and "nobody especially knew what he was going to do or how he was going to do it." Yet this very quality of disorganization was attractive. "You walked into an atmosphere of a very special kind of freedom. . . . That's the thing that is almost impossible to duplicate or find." Immediately she recognized that the factor which was making the difference was the personality of Roy Stryker. "He's not organized, but he has a hospitable mind. He has an instinct for what's important."[21] This atmosphere of freedom carried over into departmental policy, too. Lange was relieved to learn that the agency was willing to release photographs for practically any legitimate outside use. This meant that she could continue to furnish photographs to socially oriented publications such as *Survey Graphic*, just as she had done before she became a government employee.

Because she was already committed to the cause of the rural poor before she came to work for the Resettlement Administration, Dorothea Lange was relatively easy to direct. She understood the need for routine "bread and butter" pictures as well as the interpretive "photo-journalistic" photographs. If the Information Division needed a series of pictures of new house types being developed for migrant workers, or pictures of an experimental farm or camp, Lange could be counted on to deliver "straight" photographs. That is, the pictures would be sharp, clear records of the subject matter, without any sort of interpretation. Such work was hardly stimulating, yet Lange carried out these routine chores with enthusiasm because she believed in the end being sought. Sometimes it was a relief to turn from scenes of wretchedness to the neat government camps. After one such assignment,

Alabama sharecropper.
Dorothea Lange.

she wrote: "To my mind, El Monte and San Fernando Homesteads [planned rural communities] are real achievements. Especially after seeing the misery of the homeless people that I've been meeting and photographing."[22]

Dorothea Lange was completely dedicated to improving conditions for the rural poor and she was basically a cooperative person. Yet she had her foibles. These could sometimes make life interesting, if not a little difficult for Stryker. For example, Dorothea had a very strong attachment to her work. A good negative was a thing to be treasured. Like Walker Evans she was accustomed to developing all of her own film and making her own enlargements. In terms of art, this is desirable. By controlling every phase of the photographic process, from the click of the shutter to the final print, the photographer is assured that the final product, for good or ill, is his own. This very attitude—taking one's work very seriously—was what distinguished many RA and later FSA photographers from the run-of-the-mill news cameramen of the day. Certainly her attitude was in the finest tradition of Edward Weston and Ansel Adams, two photographers who had influenced her early development.[23] Yet such a protective attitude toward one's work could cause problems: it did not always fit well within the context of a government agency.

During the first two years, a great deal of time was spent trying to work out some method of accommodating the needs of the artist to the needs of the agency. These attempts were not uniformly successful. For one thing, the problem of distance was an ever present factor. Lange was working from a home base at Berkeley, California. Stryker and the historical section were in Washington. All communication had to be either by mail, which was slow and often unsatisfactory, or by much more expensive methods, telegrams or long distance telephone calls. The distance factor also meant that there would always be a time lag between when the photograph needed in Washington could be shot, processed, sent in, inspected, approved by the director, and finally released to the press or to other publications.

Lange's insistence on developing her own negatives and printing her own enlargements sometimes caused delays that lasted several weeks. Often she would be in the field for long stretches of time, saving all of her film for processing and enlarging when she returned to Berkeley. In the beginning this was not particularly damaging, but by mid-1936 the news services were beginning to make extensive use of the agency's photographs and time was becoming more and more important. Finally, there was the inescapable fact that Lange was a rather tentative darkroom technician. The mind that could grasp photographic possibilities where others saw nothing at all could not always explain why the film came out overdeveloped or the prints seemed grainy. For all of these reasons, Stryker would have preferred to have her ship her film undeveloped, directly to the laboratory in Washington, but Lange the artist and Lange the woman were to be dealt with and the process was a slow one.

In the first letter that Stryker wrote to Lange, a working arrangement was proposed. She was to develop her own negatives and make several prints of each. This done, she was to forward the negatives and one good print of each to Washington. The print that she sent would provide the "standard for later enlargements or prints made by our laboratory men here."[24] This was the arrangement that was followed on Lange's first trip for the Resettlement Administration. It should be noted that from the beginning Stryker was adamant in insisting that all negatives eventually find their way to Washington. In the early days, Lange seemed anxious to set up an elaborate laboratory at Berkeley to function as a West Coast extension of the Washington office. Stryker had to veto that idea because he knew that his budget would never stand the strain. Stryker did suggest, however, that Lange look into the possibility of hiring Ansel Adams to print her pictures.[25] (Adams was then, and is today, one of the finest darkroom men alive.) The idea of hiring Adams proved unfeasible, but by late 1936 a workable arrangement had been developed.

In order to accommodate Lange's penchant for handling all of her own film herself, Stryker decided to encourage her to set up her own darkroom at home in Berkeley. The government would share the expense of this. She was to use the darkroom to develop and print her own work and the results were to be sent to Washington for distribution. Other than her own private workshop, there was to be no elaborate facility in California, no distribution center, and no extra staff. "We can get by with getting you some material for your darkroom, supplying you with paper, chemicals, filters, and so forth," he wrote, "but to build up a staff for this work would never be approved."[26] The cooperative Lange accepted this decision gracefully. Her main interest was to advance the cause of the rural poor; within this purpose means could be somewhat flexible. After Lange's trip to Washington in 1936, there was even less friction over the handling of negatives. Once she had seen the agency at work and the good darkroom and excellent technicians that were available, her most serious misgivings over entrusting her negatives to the government disappeared.

In the cases of Evans and Lange, the exceptional quality of their

work encouraged Stryker to accommodate so far as he could their
minor eccentricities and odd work habits. With photographers
who were not productive, however, he could be quite ruthless.
During the first year of the historical section's existence, two
young photographers were briefly on the staff, neither of whom
proved adequate to the needs of the organization. The first, Paul
Carter, presented a delicate political problem because he was the
brother of John Franklin Carter who, as head of the Information
Division, was Roy Stryker's immediate superior.[27]

Paul Carter joined the staff in late 1935, bringing with him
a wealth of photographic equipment. His technical grasp of the use
of the cameras seems to have been adequate, for his pictures
were sharp and properly exposed. Unfortunately, Carter lacked
the indefinable quality which photographers call "eye." That is,
he simply did not possess the knack of seeing unusual or gripping
pictures. Further, because he was ill and overweight, Paul Carter
lacked energy and thus his trips for the historical section were
not very productive. No letters between Stryker and Carter survive
but by the end of the first year, Stryker had convinced the young
man that the life of a government photographer was not for him.
Paul, aware that his job depended on influence, relieved Roy of
embarrassment and left the agency to open up a camera store
near Dartmouth College in 1936. Roy remembered him as a "nice,
decent fellow," but of course these qualities were not enough
to justify encouraging him to remain on the staff.[28]

In the instance of Theodor Jung, Stryker appears to have held
high hopes for the photographer, only to experience bitter disap-
pointment over his failure to produce. Jung joined the agency in
September, 1935. He had been employed as a "photographic illustrator"[29] and had shown Stryker an impressive portfolio of
pictures. Once on the payroll, however, Jung had proven to have
almost no technical grasp of the camera at all. Here was precisely
the opposite of Paul Carter's problem. Jung had a fine instinct
for good pictures, but he could seldom make his camera function
at the right time.

Jung's first trip for the Resettlement Administration, in the
spring of 1936, turned into an expensive fiasco and Stryker was
quick to commit his pique to paper. In April, 1936, after Jung had
attempted several photographic assignments in the Midwest and
failed at all of them, Roy ripped out a letter that fairly scorched
the pages. "I am very much disappointed in the pictures received
from you to date," he wrote.

Hall County, Texas, 1938.
Dorothea Lange.

I am sending you two prints from your Leica negatives taken in
Cincinnati. . . . Perhaps you can diagnose your troubles better than
we can. . . . I realize that they [the prints] would look better on glossy
paper, but the fault, I am sure, lies in you and the camera, not in the
paper. . . .

Are you sure you understand the use of that camera? None of the
photographers have [*sic*] a better eye for good pictures than you do . . .
but the fault seems to lie in your camera technique.[30]

Stryker went on to point out that it cost the government some
$700 a month to keep a photographer in the field and that so far
Jung had turned in only two usable pictures. It was a long letter,
and it must have been a very hard letter for Theodor Jung to
read. Within two months he was transferred to another division
of the Resettlement Administration.[31]

Stryker could be tough, but he had to be resilient also. A major
readjustment came in the summer of 1936 when Carl Mydans
decided to leave the historical section. Mydans had been offered
a position as staff photographer with a new and exciting magazine
still in the planning stages. *Life* was being referred to as "Project
X" by those who knew about it at all. The new publishing venture
by Henry Luce had yet to see the light of day on a newsstand, but
Mydans knew that it was an opportunity which he could not afford
to let pass. Here was a chance to put into practice all that he had
learned working with Stryker. The job would certainly be more
permanent because it would not be subject to the whims of a
budget conscious Congress, and it would allow Mydans to write
as well as photograph. Because he had written for years before
becoming a full-time photographer, the chance to combine the
two media was particularly attractive.[32]

The loss of Carl Mydans created a problem for Stryker. A serious gap was left in the historical section's coverage of agricultural
problems. Arthur Rothstein was in the high plains area; Dorothea
Lange could handle the West Coast; and Walker Evans was in
the South (as nearly as could be ascertained). But what about
the problems of the rural Midwest? Jung certainly had not per-
formed impressively in that region. By the summer of 1936, Illinois and Ohio were in the grip of genuinely serious farm unrest.
Who was to cover that area? Fortunately a young man had visited
Stryker some weeks earlier in search of a job as a photographer.
His credentials seemed sound enough and therefore, shortly after
Mydans left the agency, Russell Lee was placed on the payroll.

Russell Lee was a Midwesterner himself. His family was engaged
in business and owned a considerable amount of corn land near

Mills, New Mexico, 1935.
Dorothea Lange.

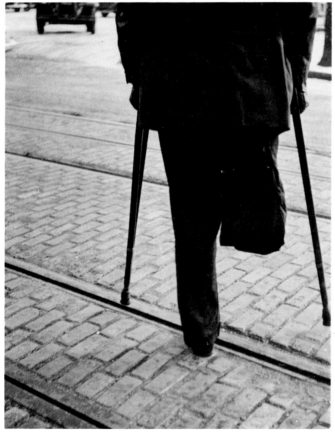

One-legged man,
1936. Theodor Jung.

79

Ottawa, Illinois. Russell had grown up in the atmosphere of small-town and rural Illinois and knew the people well. He had an uncanny ability to move into an area quietly and emerge a few days later with pictures that showed he had been completely accepted as a member of the community. His work often had a friendly "family album" quality that provided an honest contrast to some of the harsher photographic statements that other agency photographers made. Where Lange's work beseeched the onlooker to have pity on the poor, Lee's pictures seemed to say: "Look, here is a fellow who is having a hard time, but he is a decent, hard-working man and with a little help, he's going to be all right."

Lee's early training had been in the field of chemical engineering at Lehigh University. From 1925 to 1929, he had worked as a chemical engineer and plant manager for a company named "Certainteed Products." Lee had, however, become dissatisfied with the business world and had resigned in 1929 to try his hand at painting. Two years at the California School of Fine Arts plus a few years in New York convinced Lee that he was not a painter, yet he still was interested in visual representation. By 1935 he was turning to the camera. That summer he bought a Contax 35mm and began to take pictures of people and events. By now Lee and his first wife, Doris, were living at the artist colony at Woodstock, New York.[33] Doris was beginning to find markets for her painting and Russell was finding himself increasingly on the outside of things in the community.

In the early summer of 1936, a friend told him about the work that was going on in Washington. Armed with a portfolio of his work, Lee went down to the capital to see if he could fit in. He found Roy Stryker to be a pleasant man who would talk about pictures at any time of the day or night. Together they looked through his pictures of bootleg coal mining operations, estate auctions, and Father Divine on the Hudson River. Stryker seemed impressed, but there were no job openings on his staff. Lee returned to Woodstock without much hope for an assignment, but within a few weeks word came that Mydans was leaving the unit and he would be needed after all.[34]

By the fall of 1936, Lee was traveling alone through the Midwest. It was the sort of work that would make some men miserable, but he was happy. For months he lived in hotels and boarding houses, moving from one small town to the next as the needs of the agency dictated. Most of the early time was spent in Iowa, but Lee also got into Illinois, Wisconsin, Minnesota, and even parts of Michigan. From the point of view of the administrator,

Christmas dinner in
tenant farmer's home,
1936, southeastern Iowa.
Russell Lee.

Lee was a delight to work with. He seemed to be able to stay on
the road forever. He wrote long letters giving systematic plans
about where he was going and what he was doing. He used the
cameras well, seemingly at home with either large or small cameras. Best of all, he knew the region and its people.

Because Lee already knew a great deal about the farm problems
of the Midwest, Stryker dispensed with the long briefings and
simply made sure that both men were thinking along similar
lines. Before the first three months were over, Lee had rewarded
Stryker's confidence with photographs that would soon become
classics. In southwestern Iowa, Lee ran into such a scene on
Christmas Day of 1936. Four small children were attempting
to make a meal out of cornbread and a sort of thin soup. The
children were dirty and their surroundings were even worse.
The picture, together with its title, "Children Eating Christmas
Dinner," had real impact and was widely used by the news services.[35]

When Russell Lee returned to Washington in early 1937 he
quickly formed a friendship with Arthur Rothstein. Both men
loved the technical aspects of photography and enjoyed experimenting with cameras and films. Both men took an active interest
in improving the laboratory facilities, which were still relatively
primitive.[36] In the earliest days of the historical section, Arthur
Rothstein had been particularly busy with the technical aspects
of the operation. As the various technical problems were solved,
however, he began to take more and more active part in the field
photography. This was his real love and he became one of the best
of the historical section photographers.

For the young New Yorker, the chance to get out into the United States for the first time was an education in itself, and he
never missed an opportunity. In one of his earliest assignments,
Rothstein was sent to the southern mountains to photograph life
in the Appalachians. The government had recently created the
Shenandoah National Park, and the decision had been made to
purchase all privately owned land and remove the people from
the area. This would disrupt the life style of the hill people who
had lived in the area for generations. Rothstein's assignment was
to record that life style before it ceased to exist.[37] The Shenandoah
assignment in the fall of 1935 was Rothstein's first real chance
to show his former teacher that he could photograph as effectively as the more experienced members of the group. He made
thorough use of the opportunity. Using 35mm cameras to achieve
fullest flexibility, he covered every aspect of mountain life. He

Mrs. Andy Bahain, wife
of FSA client, near
Kersey, Colorado, 1939.
Arthur Rothstein. *Library
of Congress*

Cider stand, Blue Ridge
Mountains, Virginia.
Arthur Rothstein.

studied the people, got to know their ways, and returned with
pictures that were second to none.[38] Stryker must have liked what
he saw for Rothstein was soon on the road again.

During the spring and summer of 1936, Rothstein was away
from Washington almost constantly. In March he was again in
the Shenandoah Valley, this time to record the shattering effects
of a major flood.[39] By April he was in the West, taking a look at
the life of the cattle country through the eyes of a born urbanite.
In Oklahoma he was asked to try to get a picture of the effects
of dust storms on people and land. In that area, known as the Dust
Bowl, ill-considered farming techniques had combined with several years of drought to produce a terrible situation. Tons of top-
soil were being blown away by the hot summer winds and nobody
seemed to know what to do about it. While driving through Cimarron County, Oklahoma, Rothstein's eye was attracted by a fence
that was half buried by dust and sand. Seeing photographic possibilities, Arthur stopped:

> It was in Cimarron County, in the middle of the Oklahoma Pan-
> handle, that I found one of the farmers still on his land. A single cow
> stood forlornly facing away from the wind in a dusty field. The build-
> ings, barns and sheds were almost buried by drifts and in some places
> only the tops of the fenceposts could be seen. I decided to photograph
> this scene.
> While making my pictures I could hardly breathe because the dust
> was everywhere. It was so heavy in the air that the land and sky
> seemed to merge until there was no horizon. . . .
> Just as I was about to stop shooting, I saw the farmer and his two
> sons walk across the fields. As they pressed into the wind, the smallest
> child walked a few steps behind, his hands covering his eyes to protect
> them from the dust. I caught the three of them as they neared the
> shed.[40]

Whether he knew it or not, Arthur Rothstein's trip was a success at this point. The photograph he took on that dusty day became a classic, the sort of thing that would be included in every
major collection of American photographs along with Lange's
"Migrant Mother" and Walker Evans' pictures of the sharecroppers
in *Let Us Now Praise Famous Men.* The picture was used so much
that the original negative wore out long ago and recent reproduc-
tions of "Dust Storm, Cimarron Co., 1936" have had to be made
from copies.

Rothstein's western trip took him north from Oklahoma into
the big ranch country. Stryker had spent a great deal of time preparing his young protégé for this part of his journey. He had been
given books to read; he had been introduced to cattlemen and
western agricultural experts. He had prepared shooting scripts

Outhouse on farm, Cim-
arron County, Oklahoma,
1936. Arthur Rothstein.
Library of Congress

Dust storm, Cimarron
County, Oklahoma, 1936.
Arthur Rothstein.

and carried the usual pamphlets and maps. Arthur had never seen a cattle roundup before, but he knew exactly what to expect. In Montana he captured the details of roundup time with the subtlety of a man who had spent his life working on the range. In the sheep country, his pictures captured the loneliness of the solitary herders and the spaciousness of the land on which they lived. The pictures kept rolling into Washington, and Roy continued to grow more and more pleased with Arthur's results.

In late April, 1936, Arthur was in North Dakota looking for pictures that might later prove useful. Much of his assigned work had been completed and there was time left to look for good photographs. Near Fargo he ran into a scene that seemed to have some possibilities. Beside the road was an alkali flat, barren and parched. It seemed to symbolize drought conditions. There was even an old steer skull nearby to provide just the needed mournful touch. The artist in Rothstein was aroused. He spent quite a while with the little plot of parched ground and the skull, moving the ancient artifact from one position to another, looking for good lighting effects and angles. In the end he had five photographs. Several showed the skull on cracked earth; several showed it on the edge of a grassy rise of land. All were taken within a ten- or fifteen-foot radius. The pictures were duly developed and mailed off to Washington where they were enthusiastically received. Roy liked them so well that he dashed off a letter to Arthur specifically congratulating him on the series.[41] Nobody thought anything more about the incident—for the time being. The pictures were released to the press and were used by newspapers all over the country. Everyone seemed to like the shots.

A few months later, the steer skull pictures were the center of a storm of controversy. The ax fell in August, 1936, an election year and a year in which the Republican forces in the Midwest were looking desperately for any issue that could possibly embarrass the Roosevelt administration. The imbroglio developed over the drought issue on the high plains. By the summer of 1936, serious drought had engulfed middle America, and conditions in the Dust Bowl were worse than anyone could remember. Roosevelt decided to send a delegation of farm experts to tour the area on a fact-finding mission. His action was probably politically motivated, like most maneuvers of this sort. Roosevelt was using the opportunity to show his concern for agriculture. The drought tour, led by Tugwell of the Resettlement Administration, was to cover a five-state area of the high plains. It was to begin in Oklahoma and move through western Kansas, Nebraska, and into the

South Dakota Badlands,
"The Skull," 1936.
Arthur Rothstein.

Dakotas. The President himself was scheduled to come West during the latter part of the tour and meet the group at Bismarck, North Dakota. At that point, supposedly, some sort of conclusion could be drawn as to the proper role for the federal government to play in alleviating the Dust Bowl conditions.[42]

The trip received a tremendous amount of publicity. Many papers published maps showing the precise route of the drought commission. Each new discovery of bad rural conditions received the full measure of press treatment. In an area that was staunchly Republican and proud, the revelations of bad living and farming conditions were extremely unpopular. Many saw the entire matter in political terms and heartily wished that the Democrats would take their social concern elsewhere. In Fargo, North Dakota, the editor of the *Forum,* a Republican newspaper, found an issue that seemed to have the possibility of turning the tour and the President's western trip into a shambles. Seizing happily on the matter, the paper laid a trap for the President and the Resettlement Administration.

On the morning of August 27, 1936, the *Forum* carried a front-page story branding Rothstein's skull photographs "phony pictures." Under a headline, "It's A Fake," the writer noted that Rothstein had moved the skull around the alkali flat and had shot it on both the parched earth and the grassy hillock. The article also insisted that the skull had obviously been bleaching for years and was not therefore a product of recent conditions. Finally, the article noted that the picture had been taken in the spring, before the actual drought conditions had occurred.[43] The paper was somehow smuggled aboard the presidential train on the day that it entered North Dakota and hundreds of copies were distributed to the newsmen and politicians aboard. The story created quite a sensation. The clear implication of the story was that the skull was a mobile prop that Rothstein carried around with him and used to create a mournful mood in any picture he took. "Listen, Mr. Easterner," the article trumpeted, "may we suggest in all friendliness, that while you are in these parts, you take no wooden nickel pictures like this."[44]

The story of faked pictures by a Resettlement Administration photographer made good copy and was quickly picked up by many of the major newspapers on the East Coast. The New York *Herald Tribune* and the New York *Sun* both carried the story. It was even picked up by the news services and carried in smaller papers all over the country.[45] Soon the integrity of other photographs was under question. Then it was simple to question the integrity

Driving cattle, Custer Forest, Montana,
1939. Arthur Rothstein.

Sheepherder's wagon on
US 30, Sweetwater
County, Wyoming, 1940.
Arthur Rothstein.

of the entire agency and its aims. The low point was achieved by
the Erie, Pennsylvania, *Dispatch-Herald:*

> The revelation that Dr. Rexford Tugwell's "Resettlement Admin-
> istration," the principal socialistic experiment of the New Deal, has
> been guilty of . . . flagrantly faked "drought" pictures, designed to give
> the public an exaggerated idea of the amount of damage done by the
> lack of rainfall, is a highly instructive, but not especially surprising
> development.
>
> The whole resettlement program is a ghastly fake, based on fake
> ideas, and what is more natural than that it should be promoted by
> fake methods similar to those used by ordinary confidence men.[46]

In Washington, the office of the historical section was thrown
into some confusion. Stryker was out of town when the trouble
hit and, thus, full responsibility fell on Edwin Locke, a young
man who had recently joined the section as Stryker's assistant.[47]
Locke did the best he could. He issued a statement exonerating
Rothstein and defending the right of the photographer to make
minor changes in the scene in order to increase the graphic impact of a picture. "Every newspaper or photographic agency usually takes several shots of similar views in order to insure having
one or two good photographs," Locke wrote. "This is good photographic practice and one which the Resettlement Administration
will continue."[48] In a hurried note to Rothstein, who was still
on the road, however, the young assistant sounded considerably
less sure of himself: "Look at the clipping and look at the rebuttal,
and also look in your current newspapers for an A.P. story in
which I deny the spuriousness of our photography. They will
probably try to get in touch with you if this matter goes any
further, so if you still have that goddam skull, hide it for Christ's
sake. Stick close to my story."[49]

Shortly after Locke's note to Rothstein, Stryker returned to
Washington and began putting the pieces together again. The
Herald Tribune was eventually satisfied that the agency did not
make a practice of faking photographs, and it printed a retraction
that was picked up by a few of the midwestern newspapers that
had run the original story.[50] Most of the papers, however, ignored
it. For years people in the Midwest would associate the Resettlement Administration with "faked" pictures.[51] In Washington no
one placed any blame at all on Arthur Rothstein. The situation
had certainly not been one of his making. He had gone West to
take pictures of drought conditions and had succeeded in symbol-
izing the problem in a series of powerful photographs. In 1937
the influential photography magazine, *U. S. Camera,* honored

Death Valley, California.
Arthur Rothstein.

Rothstein's skull pictures as among the best of the year.[52] Even so, from the standpoint of politics, a certain amount of damage had been done to the agency and its photographic division by the editor of the Fargo *Forum.*

The latter part of 1936 was a difficult period for Roy Stryker and his photographers. In the midst of the newspaper controversy concerning government photographic propaganda, the original Director of Information, John Franklin Carter, left to take a more lucrative job. His replacement was a man who had little use for photographs or photographers and used every opportunity to weaken the historical section.[53] For Stryker this change meant that he faced months of political infighting merely to keep his project alive. In the fall two sudden announcements came. Roy was to cut down on the size of his photographic staff, and, worst of all, Rexford Tugwell was leaving government service. Again Stryker considered resigning. Eventually, of course, he decided to stay and fight for his agency. The project was worth saving, even if it meant the loss of personnel or even some compromise in aims and directions.

During September and October, 1936, Roy reshuffled his entire operation. Evans was still on leave, working with Agee on *Let Us Now Praise Famous Men,* so he did not have to be figured into the budget cuts. Even so, one photographer would have to leave the payroll. After a period of agonizing indecision, Stryker knew that the person to be dropped would have to be Dorothea Lange. She was one of his best. She was cooperative and enthusiastic, but she would have to be the victim. In the final analysis, the process of attempting to correlate the work of the Washington office with a photographer who was permanently based on the West Coast had simply proven too burdensome and expensive. The physical problems of getting negatives back and forth, sending supplies from Washington to California, and keeping up the extensive correspondence required turned out to be greater than Roy had anticipated. From an administrative standpoint, the choice was clear.

In early October, 1936, Roy sadly wrote Dorothea that she was going to have to leave the staff. He was careful to make clear that there was no implied dissatisfaction with her work. In fact he was quite bitter at the leadership of the Information Division because of the budget cuts that had made the trimming necessary. "I am now down to two photographers, Rothstein and [Lee]," he wrote. "They will be kept here in Washington and their work will be primarily of the news information type."[54] For solace Stryker

Blue Ridge mountaineer
peeling apples, Virginia.
Arthur Rothstein.

offered to try to keep Lange in the agency on a short term *(per diem)* basis and promised that as soon as the political skies cleared a bit, she would be back on the regular payroll. The implication was clear: Roy was going to fight as long as he could.

For the next two months, a quiet but grim battle went on in the Washington office of the Information Division. Stryker's object was to retain Lange as long as he could with little money and no support from above. First, she was given her two weeks furlough, then the two weeks of sick leave that she had accumulated. When that ran out, small projects that could be done on a *per diem* basis were found. In late October, 1936, Roy wrote Lange a friendly (if somewhat conspiratorial) letter, outlining his strategy. "Get all set for your job at the migrant camps. I am asking for two weeks for you to do the work. Then, after the two weeks have been allotted, I will inform them that after all you have to develop and print the stuff, for which I shall have to ask for additional time. You may look for another note along in a couple of days with definite approval on this."[55]

Eventually time came to the rescue. In early 1937 the Resettlement Administration was transferred from independent status to the Department of Agriculture. In the major reshuffle that accompanied the change, the Director of Information who had been the source of most of Stryker's troubles was transferred to other work. The new director proved more sympathetic; Lange was back on the payroll by the end of January. Things were returning to normal.[56]

By the spring of 1937, Stryker had become a seasoned veteran of New Deal Washington. He knew how to direct photographers and he knew how to fight their battles for them. He was learning to meet some matters head on and to retreat when he had to. By now his guidance had become quite sure. He would miss his old friend Rexford Tugwell. He would often be frustrated by the new adjustments necessitated by the transfer to the Department of Agriculture. But Stryker would no longer need special protection within the agency. He knew his way around and he had proved the worth of his approach. Hundreds of the pictures that the historical section had produced had already found their way into magazines and books. There had been criticism, of course, but it had been mostly of a partisan nature, the product of the overheated environment of an election year. All things considered, the project had developed well in its first two years and was fully prepared for the challenges that lay ahead.

V

A Time of
Broadening

The later years of the Farm Security Administration's historical section were a time of broadening. From 1937 until the demise of the project in 1942, Roy Stryker and his staff were moving out in new directions, looking for better ways to explain to the American people the problems of rural poverty, and attempting to tell more and more of the whole story of the United States during the depression. During this period new pictorial emphases appeared. The photographers and their director became interested in the small town as a center of rural life and even extended their interest to the city. They recognized that many rural people were moving to urban centers, bringing rural problems and attitudes with them.

By mid-1937 a series of bureaucratic attacks on the historical section had been weathered, and a more peaceful and productive atmosphere existed in the Washington office. Several factors contributed to this change. Primary among them was the transformation of the Resettlement Administration from an independent agency, created by presidential order, to a duly constituted agency within the United States Department of Agriculture. The RA was taken into that department in early 1937. By the end of that year, it had been given legal status under the Bankhead-Jones Farm Tenancy Act. The Bankhead-Jones Act also changed the name of the RA to the Farm Security Administration. The transfer to the Department of Agriculture, along with Tugwell's resignation, had filled Stryker with dread when it was first announced in late 1936, but it appears to have worked to the advantage of the photographic project.[1]

The absorption of the Resettlement Administration's activities into the department tended to make the agency's personnel more acceptable, both to the bureaucratic corps in Washington and to the farmers in the country. Resettlement was now somewhat more "legitimate."[2] Furthermore the move to agriculture did not necessarily mean that the group would be swallowed up or that its programs would be subverted. Before leaving his position as director of the RA, Tugwell had satisfied himself that his programs to aid rural poor had powerful friends in the Department of Agriculture. He had spent a great deal of time and effort insuring the sympathy of Secretary of Agriculture Henry Wallace. He had even gotten Wallace to accompany him on a trip through the South to observe Resettlement Administration projects in action. Wallace had been impressed with what he saw.[3] Thereafter he would support projects to aid the rural poor. Milburn L. Wilson, one of the men who designed the original AAA program, was still in the Department of Agriculture and was strongly interested in the work that the agency had been doing. Milton Eisenhower, Chief of the Information Division of the Department of Agriculture, was a long-time friend of Stryker's. In time of need, Stryker would still find sympathetic ears in the offices above his.[4]

Tugwell's decision to step down may have made life easier for the Resettlement Administration in some respects. He had become a personal symbol of everything that powerful farm bloc conservatives in Washington hated. He had become a political "lightning rod," a target for those who feared government experimentation. As such, his replacement by the comparatively noncontroversial Dr. Will Alexander tended to make the entire resettlement project somewhat more palatable to those who saw it as a socialistic plot to communize the American farmer.[5]

Finally, the historical section was undergoing certain changes in its own emphasis that would tend to broaden its appeal. Stryker and his photographers were becoming increasingly interested in the larger outlines of American life. As they turned their cameras on a broader range of subjects, they appealed to a larger segment of the population. During the first two years, the photographers had looked unblinkingly at the worst of rural poverty. Now the time had come to consider other areas—rural, small-town, and even urban life.

In the spring of 1936, a conversation with a famous urban sociologist set Stryker's mind on new directions of exploration. Stryker had taken the train to New York City to spend the day with his old friend Robert Lynd, author of the important Middletown study.[6] The two had lunch together and Stryker brought out a large batch of photographs to show Lynd what his project was accomplishing. Lynd was quite impressed with what he saw. The possibility of using photographs to show sociological or his-

Elgin, Illinois, 1941. John Vachon. *Library of Congress*

Women of congregation of Wheeley's church, with brooms and buckets on annual Cleanup Day, Gordonton, North Carolina, 1939. Dorothea Lange.

torical points had not occurred to him. In his enthusiasm Lynd's
mind ran ahead to grasp new possibilities. What about a photographic study of small-town life in America?[7] Here was a life style
related directly to rural problems, one that was slipping away and
would soon be lost. What were the factors that distinguished the
life patterns of small-town America?

The two men sat for hours after lunch at the Columbia University faculty club, talking excitedly. When it was time to catch the
night train back to Washington, Roy's mind was seething with
ideas. During the trip he sat with a large pad of notebook paper
and made notes of everything he could remember from the conversation. By the time he reached Washington, the pad was filled.[8]

In order to systematize his attempt to document life in small
towns, Stryker adopted an almost Socratic method. His ideas were
put in the form of questions. What do people do at home in the
evenings? Do the activities in a small town differ from those in
a large city? Do they vary according to income groups? How do
various income levels dress when they go to church? Where do
people meet? Do beer halls and pool halls take the place of country
clubs for the poor? Do women of lower income levels have as
many opportunities for social mixing as their wealthier counter-
parts? Are there differences in the way people of the same social
level look and dress in small towns as opposed to larger cities?
Is it more necessary for middle income people to keep up a neat
and polished appearance in large cities than in small towns?[9]

Pushing questions of this sort even further, Stryker began to
ask himself broader questions about small-town USA. What are
the key economic factors in the existence of a small town? The
railroad? The highway? How can these be represented visually?
Has anyone ever taken a really good series of pictures of a filling
station, showing its relationship to the restless, shifting American
population? What do railroad stations look like? How do they
relate to small-town life?[10]

By the summer of 1936, thinking of this sort had given rise to
a whole new series of suggestions to photographers in the form
of several shooting scripts. Stryker and his photographers had
worked out many shooting scripts before. In fact it had become
standard practice for a photographer going into the field to have
a study sheet from the chief with suggestions of pictures and
source books. Even so, there had never been a series of scripts
quite like the one on small-town America. It was broad and it was
detailed. By the end of the summer, it was developed, and by early
1937 results were beginning to appear.

Mining settlement, Scott's Run, West Virginia,
1935. Walker Evans.

Main Street store fronts,
Edwards, Mississippi,
1936. Walker Evans.

The photographers soon learned to keep an eye open for pictures that might fit into the small-town project. There was seldom money to send a man out just to work on small towns, but if pictures presented themselves, they were taken. When Arthur Rothstein was in Montana working on pictures of a sheep ranch, he was expected to look for pictures that would catch the essence of a small Montana town. Other photographers did the same sort of thing. Many of these pictures were not matters of immediate need. Often they did not relate directly to the work of the Farm Security Administration. Nevertheless, Stryker's instincts told him that they were an important part of the overall record of life in the 1930s, and he continued to encourage his people to get such pictures as often as possible.

The shift of interest to include small towns was significant in several ways. It meant that the historical section was becoming more than a simple propaganda agency for a farm program and was moving toward a broader interpretation of its own role. It meant that Stryker and the others were coming to realize that the farm problem was moving to the cities, as more and more country people, uprooted and without urban skills, were forced off the land and into a town or city environment. This realization and the widening view of American culture that it produced vastly increased the usefulness of the photographic files for later historians, sociologists, and others who would need to know what the United States looked like during the depression years. The broadening of interests also enhanced the usefulness of the file to contemporaries. Magazines and news services had already become accustomed to turning to Washington for excellent pictures of rural poverty or distress. Now they would learn to look there for pictures of the small town and even the emerging urban profile.

One of the earliest results of the shift in interest was a book by Sherwood Anderson titled *Home Town*.[11] Anderson, who was at work on a series called "The Face of America," was approached by the Farm Security Administration in 1939 with the idea of using some of its small-town pictures to illustrate a book. The idea came from Edwin Rosskam, a recently hired addition to the Washington staff specializing in layout and photoediting. Anderson liked the idea and agreed to cooperate. Rosskam was to aid in the selection of the pictures and Anderson was to supply the text. The job turned into a major operation for Rosskam when Anderson's proposed text, 70,000 words in length, arrived. The publisher had asked for 20,000! Rosskam was left with the respon-

Signs along highway,
Green County, Georgia,
1937. Marion Post Wol-
cott. *Library of Congress*

Charleston, West Vir-
ginia, 1938. Marion Post
Wolcott. *Library of
Congress*

sibility of paring down the text as well as supplying the pictures.[12] In terms of official credit, the book remained Anderson's although Rosskam had certainly played a key editorial role in its development. Later Rosskam would be able to garner some credits of his own when he teamed up with Negro writer Richard Wright and photographer Russell Lee to produce a book on urban Negro problems titled *Twelve Million Black Voices*.[13]

While they moved into the area of urban and small-town documentation, the FSA photographers could never ignore their usual work with rural problems. This might take the form of a special investigation into some specific farm problem, such as hookworm in the South or hunger in California. Occasionally it might mean that FSA photographers actually covered an event that affected large portions of the rural population. The group never functioned as a news agency, but a natural disaster or a major national change could sometimes force them to work in some of the same ways that newsmen did. On such occasions, however, their way of covering the event was quite different from the average newsman's. In the case of a natural disaster, their concern was with long-term effects on men and land, not so much with immediate events. A good example of such a case occurred in February, 1937, when major floods inundated the Ohio and Mississippi River valleys. These were events which affected large numbers of farmers and so the FSA was involved.

Walker Evans, with Ed Locke sent along to keep track of his whereabouts, was to circulate in the area of the Lower Mississippi. Both were instructed to record the aftermath of the flooding. While news photographers took pictures of rising waters ripping houses apart and men piling sandbags against the river, the FSA men turned their cameras on the human side of the story and the effects of the water on the land.

Evans and Locke spent most of their time along the levees in Arkansas. There, in the makeshift camps set up for the displaced flood victims, they recorded a stark impression of human misery. Eastern-born and raised, Locke was surprised and shocked to find that the displaced Negroes in the refugee camps were not "happy-go-lucky about it, but dazed, apathetic and hopeless."[14] Like many city people of his day, Locke had had little contact with Negroes and had fallen victim to minstrel show stereotypes. Evans, utterly familiar with the southern scene, worked well and Stryker professed to be pleased with the results.[15]

While Evans and Locke worked the levees, Russell Lee covered the Ohio Valley. His assignment was to wait until the crest of

Sign on land near Iron
River, Michigan, 1937.
Russell Lee.

the floodwaters had passed and record the effects.[16] His pictures
reflected deep sympathy for the people and feeling for the land.
The flood story was only Lee's second assignment for Stryker,
but the people in Washington were becoming increasingly aware
of his steady competency. By the spring of 1937, Lee had been
on the road constantly since late October of the previous year.
He had not even had time to get to Washington to look through
the files. Like Dorothea Lange he had simply been sent out into
the field to produce, and like Lange he was producing. Long letters
kept him in touch with Washington, and Stryker made sure that
each batch of pictures received in the office was processed as
quickly as possible and brought to him so that Lee could have
the benefit of his comments by return mail. In this way he could
continue to direct the work of the young man he had met only
briefly.

After the effects of flooding had been recorded, Lee turned
northward and headed for Wisconsin and Minnesota. In that area
poor farmers had been victimized by unscrupulous timber com-
panies that had stripped all vegetation from the land and then
sold it (often sight unseen) to families for farming purposes.
These cutover lands were usually unsuitable for any sort of agriculture and were subject to the worst sort of erosion. Nevertheless
there were families in the region who were trying to make the
lands pay. Lee went North to see how they were doing and to
give some publicity to their plight.[17]

On his way into the cutover country, Lee met Roy Stryker at
Duluth. The director had come out to the Midwest on one of his
rare visits to the photographer in the field. Perhaps he had de-
spaired of ever getting Lee back to Washington. Perhaps he just
wanted to see one of his men in action, but most likely he simply
wanted to get out of Washington for a while and felt the need to
discuss pictures with Lee.

The two men traveled together to Minneapolis and Madison.
They talked endlessly for several days. Stryker had brought along
a large batch of Lee's pictures for the photographer to look over.
It was the first time that Lee had seen any of the work that he
was doing for the FSA.[18] Together the two men went through
the pictures. Stryker pointed out strengths and weaknesses. Lee
listened. Later, they went out into the field and it was the chief's
turn to watch and listen. What he saw impressed him. Lee had
a knack for talking to people that few persons possessed. Stryker
came away from the visit with new respect for the young man.[19]

When the job in the cutover country was finished, Lee was

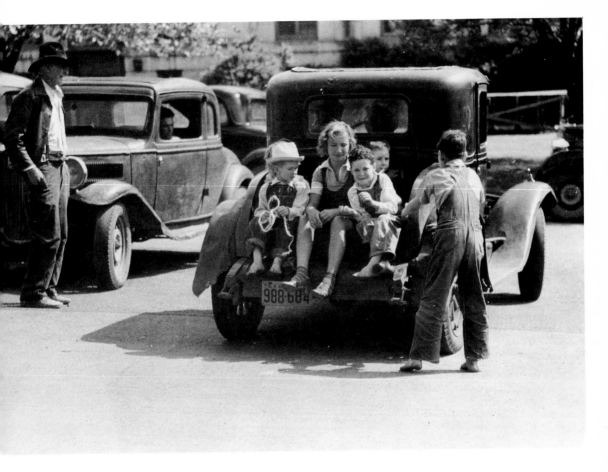

San Augustine, Texas,
1939. Russell Lee.
Library of Congress

John Adams, home-
steader, drags ties down
from mountains with
burros to get cash for
his farm, Pie Town, New
Mexico, 1940. Russell
Lee. *Library of Congress*

105

finally brought back to the Washington home office. It was his first visit to Washington since he joined the staff. He had been on the road continuously nearly eight months. During the summer of 1937, Lee relaxed, puttered in the lab with Arthur Rothstein, absorbed the hospitality of the Stryker home, fattened on Alice's good cooking, and in general had a fine time. In the fall he returned to the field.[20]

In the final months of the year, another money crisis had to be weathered. President Roosevelt had decided that the time had come to try to cut down on government spending. He believed that the economy had reached a point in its development where additional government spending added a burden rather than improving the chances for economic growth. As one of his advisors put it, it was time to "tear off the bandages and throw away the crutches" and see if the economy could stand by itself.[21] Accordingly the money allotted for the major relief programs was drastically reduced. The roles of such work projects as the WPA (Works Progress Administration) were cut back sharply. Roosevelt and his advisors were convinced that private business could employ the men who were cut off the relief roles.

The experiment failed. The economy was not able to absorb the shock and a major economic setback gripped the entire country. One result of the so-called "Roosevelt Recession" was that Roy Stryker had considerably less money to spend during the latter part of 1937 and early 1938. Walker Evans, who had lost interest in the project and had become something of a personal trial to Stryker, was taken off the payroll in September.[22] In October the long-suffering Dorothea Lange again left the staff temporarily and the agency was trimmed to the bone.[23] Again the burden fell on Arthur Rothstein and Russell Lee.

For months the historical section did relatively little of the documentary work that Stryker and the photographers enjoyed. Instead most of the time was devoted to mundane illustrative pictures for the Department of Agriculture and work for outside agencies. The department always seemed to need more pictures of ladies canning fruit or men building better hog pens. The Department of Public Health discovered that FSA photographers delivered first-rate pictures with a minimum of fuss and began to use their services regularly. This was not exactly what Stryker had had in mind when he came to Washington, but it was work, and the health department paid its bills on time, and the historical section needed money. In the summer of 1938, Rothstein did extensive work for Public Health.

Montana cowboy.
Arthur Rothstein.

Sometimes a trip to photograph a distant Public Health project could be used to pay for a project closer to the hearts of Stryker and his photographers. For example, that summer Rothstein traveled extensively in the Midwest, almost completely at the expense of Public Health. He filmed a project for that department in Peoria, Illinois, and another in Indianapolis. While he was doing these chores, he was also able to go to Vincennes, Indiana, to photograph an FSA co-op in action. On his way home, he swung south and was able to get some effective documentary photographs of the coal mining districts of Kentucky and West Virginia.[24]

In the same way, Russell Lee was sent to Hot Springs, Arkansas, to photograph a Public Health project in September, 1938.[25] While he was there, word came through that Public Health wanted him to go to New Orleans when the work in Hot Springs was finished. The trip evolved into one of the most successful that Lee made. He had six weeks to cover health projects in New Orleans, plenty of time to get out into the countryside and document the rural life of southern Louisiana.[26] While in New Orleans, he met a bright young newspaperwoman from Dallas, Texas, named Jean Smith. The two immediately discovered mutual interests and began to work together. Within a year and a half, Jean would be the second Mrs. Russell Lee.[27]

By the latter part of September, Lee had finished most of the work that Public Health had for him to do in the New Orleans area, but he was not ready to leave. He wrote Stryker asking for time to attend the National Rice Festival in early October. "This really sounds like something," he wrote. "Cajun dances, Cajun bands, balls and all sorts of ceremonies, big parades and floats. Please do not commit me for any work from October 3 to October 6, because I certainly want to attend this."[28]

In such ways, by keeping alert for good subjects to photograph while carrying out routine assignments for other agencies, FSA photographers were able to continue the work of documenting American life, even during periods when there was little or no money in the budget for "frills" such as recording the American scene.

Like the swing of a pendulum, times returned to normal for the agency and the historical section by the end of 1938. Convinced of their errors, Roosevelt and his advisors restored the projects to undergird the economy, and gradually government and private spending began to rise.[29] By October Dorothea Lange was back on the payroll and a new photographer had been hired. Marion Post, an attractive and determined young woman, had

Barker at concession,
state fair, Donaldsonville,
Louisiana, 1938.
Russell Lee.

Fortune teller,
Donaldsonville,
Louisiana, 1938.
Russell Lee.

109

the ability to capture pictures that were lyrics of the land. Her eye reflected a deep love for the good earth.

Marion Post was a city girl. The product of a fashionable home, she had attended New York University and the New School for Social Research in New York City. To round out her education in proper style she had studied at the University of Vienna.[30] While in Vienna Marion had come in contact with photography for the first time and even purchased a small Rollei camera for her own amusement. At this point there was no consideration of a career in photography. It was simply a side interest.

Once again in New York, Marion took a job at the progressive private school, Croton-on-Hudson. It was a good job, but her interest in photography continued and grew. Sometime in mid-1936 she joined the staff of the Philadelphia *Evening Bulletin,* doing feature and fashion work, usually from the woman's angle. Again, it was a good job, but it was not exactly what she had had in mind. During the years in Europe, she had come in contact with the liberal ideology and its imprint remained. Now she wanted to use her cameras to report on more important things than garden parties. After a year and a half with the *Evening Bulletin,* she approached an old friend, New York photographer Ralph Steiner, and asked him if he knew of any interesting projects that needed a photographer. When Steiner told her of Stryker's work in Washington, Marion decided to look into the project.

Armed with a letter from Steiner, Miss Post went to the capital city. Her timing was perfect. She arrived in late 1938, just as Stryker was considering enlarging the staff. He inspected the portfolio of her work that she had brought, while she looked over the FSA files; both parties were impressed. In a few weeks she found herself a government employee.[31]

Marion Post's near-romantic view of the countryside became evident immediately. The city girl reacted to the country in somewhat the same way that Arthur Rothstein had in the early days. Her ability to take pictures that spoke of rural beauty and fertility fitted well with a new direction that the historical section was taking in late 1938. During that year Stryker had begun to question the policy of emphasizing only the lower third of the agricultural community. The beginnings of change seem to have come during one of his periodic visits to New York City.

Stryker had dropped by the offices of *Survey Graphic,* probably to show some recent pictures, and he fell into conversation with Mrs. Paul Kellogg, wife of the magazine's editor. Mrs. Kellogg had recently received a letter from a farmer in upstate New York

Shenandoah Valley,
Virginia. Marion Post
Wolcott.

that had set her mind onto a new line of thought. The farmer
had pointed out that the pictures in *Survey Graphic* created a
false impression of farm life. By concentrating on the lower third
of the farm population, the pictures and articles in the magazine
tended to reverse national concepts with regard to farmers. Urban
people who had earlier believed that farmers had no problems
were now becoming convinced that all farmers lived like animals.
Neither extreme was true. In fact the problem of rural poverty
was in real danger of being oversold. Mrs. Kellogg thought that
the farmer had made an accurate criticism. After considering
the matter, Stryker had to agree.[32] After the summer of 1938, the
work of the FSA photographers began to move consciously into
the positive aspects of rural life. More pictures were taken of
the lush countryside of New England in summer, for example.
(Marion Post made several trips into the area in both summer
and winter.) Less work of a directly propagandistic nature was
done. In the years after 1938, emphasis shifted to include a more
balanced view of rural life.

As they grew more sophisticated in their grasp of rural life
in the United States, FSA photographers began to provide more
than just pictures. Stryker had always encouraged them to report
fully any problems that they ran into and thus, in time, they became reporters. Like a series of sensitive meters scattered around
the country, the photographic staff could be depended upon to
know where rural unrest was building up or where miners were
becoming seriously discontented. This information, added to that
supplied by other USDA field representatives, helped to form a
clear picture in Washington of what new programs might be
needed in the future.

Sometimes the situation reported dealt with subtle problems
of adjustment within the already existing farm programs. In 1939
Arthur Rothstein, who was in the Midwest, reported that all the
corn farmers in the region were selling their produce to the government. "As a result the price of corn on spot delivery is going
up rapidly and some farmers are even having trouble getting feed
for their livestock. Maybe the ever-normal granary is working too
well?"[33]

More often, however, the problem was quite specific and dealt
with a particular injustice. In 1937 the local California representative of the Resettlement Administration (before the name change)
was in trouble with the power structure of the Imperial Valley.
At issue was the matter of migrant camps. The government wanted to establish one in the area, but landowners preferred to keep

Barbourville, Kentucky,
1940. Marion Post Wolcott.

Drift fence and farmland from
Sugar Hill, near Franconia,
New Hampshire, 1940.
Marion Post Wolcott.

control of labor in their own hands. Dorothea Lange wrote to Stryker asking permission to go into the area and giving an insider's assessment of what was going on. She said:

> What goes on in the Imperial Valley is beyond belief. The . . . valley has a social structure all its own and partly because of its isolation in the state those in control get away with it. . . . The R.A. has decided to make a crack into the valley affairs by putting up a camp. Those in control are bitterly opposed and there is trouble ahead. Garst [Jonathan Garst, Regional Director for California] went down there last week . . . and says that he "ran into a hurricane." Down there if they don't like you they shoot you and give you the works . . . beat you up and dump you in a ditch at the county line. . . . In other words it's a hot spot and for R.A. to go in is a dramatic situation. We shall need pictures. They are bringing all kinds of pressure to stop it.[34]

Within a few weeks, Lange received permission to go into the Imperial Valley. Her pictures became a part of the campaign which eventually brought decent, government-run camps for migrants throughout California.

One of the most serious situations that Arthur Rothstein encountered occurred in the Midwest on the trip in 1939. He had gone West to visit the ranch country again. The shooting script that he carried along called for detailed coverage of all phases of the cattle industry. The emphasis was to be on the positive aspects of cattle work, including the beauty of the land and the strength of the people. Before he reached his goal, however, he unearthed an ugly situation in the vicinity of Herrin, Illinois. Here, in the commercial farming district, the sharecrop system was under attack; evicted people were camping along the highways. Furthermore local officials were contributing to increased unrest. Newspapers in the Herrin area had attempted to lay the blame for all troubles on the Triple A and Henry Wallace, but Rothstein reported that this was a conscious distortion of the facts: "The situation was created when the planters gave the 'croppers' the alternative of getting off the land or remaining as day laborers, paying rent in cash and existing . . . just as the miners here exist in the company towns. The move to the highways was a public protest against this kind of economic slavery."

Rothstein reported that the local officials had systematically weeded out the leaders of the protest movement and had sent them out of town, leaving the remainder lost and bewildered: "They are much worse off now than they were before. . . . While they were along the roads people brought them food and clothing, although the Red Cross refused to do anything under threats . . . from the local planters. . . . But the state troopers moved them

State Highway officials
moving sharecroppers,
New Madrid County, Missouri,
1939. Arthur Rothstein,
Library of Congress.

Evicted sharecropper and
child, New Madrid
County, Missouri, 1939.
Arthur Rothstein. *Library
of Congress*

from the highway. . . . Most of them are now in open fields or barns, well away from the public eye."

Rothstein went on to report that public officials were actually trying to force the sharecroppers to break the law so that they could be legally prosecuted. About seventy-five families of poor Negroes had been moved into a section along the river inhabited by the roughest element of whites. "It was obviously an attempt to incite a race riot on the part of the local police who would then blame it all on communists. This may happen in the next few days unless they are moved again."[35]

Rothstein's letter was some of the first evidence that reached the main office of the FSA concerning the sharecropper strike that began in January, 1937. It had begun in the Missouri "boot-heel" area and spread into Illinois. Under the urging of Rothstein and other interested parties, the FSA sent tents, food, and medical personnel to help alleviate the suffering. Later, it carried out an effective project to provide housing for six hundred displaced families.[36]

Occasionally, an FSA photographer might find himself embroiled directly with local authorities. In March, 1937, Rothstein ran into a situation as dangerous as any that an FSA photographer ever faced. He had gone South to photograph living and working conditions around the mines in the Birmingham, Alabama, area. At this time the owners of the mines were anxious to avoid unfavorable publicity and union trouble, and a certain nervousness had arisen about strangers with cameras. Rothstein had gone to the Red Ore Mine of the Tennessee Coal and Iron Company when trouble broke out:

> I . . . started to take pictures of the place. Just as I was about to get a shot of one of their hundred armed deputies, a car tried to run me over. One of the mine foremen got out swearing and took Tom [Hibbon, a companion] and me into custody. Everybody was excited—someone would have thought we had tried to blow up the mine. Men with shotguns surrounded us and we had to do a lot of fast explaining to the mine superintendent before he would let us go. If either of us had been alone, I suppose the story would have been different.[37]

Although almost every FSA photographer had similar experiences, such incidents were exceptional. Usually Stryker's staff could count on excellent cooperation.

The agency's cameras could be critical of situations that were created by unjust men or systems, but they could also show warm approval in other instances. Marion Post's romantic pictures of the Vermont landscape show this. Even better examples come from the work of Russell Lee.

Oldtimers near courthouse, San Augustine, Texas,
1939. Russell Lee. *Library of Congress*

San Augustine, Texas,
1939. Russell Lee. *Library
of Congress*

In late April, 1939, Lee reported that he and Jean were interested in a small Texas town named San Augustine. They had come to the area to do a story on the effects of hookworm and had become interested in the community for its own sake. Lee found San Augustine to be a beautiful village where many of the old patterns of small-town life could still be clearly seen. The town square was a political center and market. The school served as a place of education and a meeting house. The people retained the small town modes of life in a very pure form. One could still find general stores and old-fashioned shops. Cattle sales were held periodically. The architecture of the village was in the very best nineteenth century traditions. Lee loved it all, and it was a perfect place to do a major documentary on small-town life as it related to an agricultural area.[38] Russell and Jean spent less than a week in San Augustine, but when they were through, Lee had one of the finest sets of pictures that he would make for FSA.

Almost exactly a year later, Russell and Jean produced a second set of pictures that illustrated Lee's deep love of the land and rural people. In April, 1940, on a trip through New Mexico, the couple became fascinated with a name on their map. A community called "Pie Town" certainly seemed worth investigating! They finally found the hamlet with the strange name, well off the beaten path. Pie Town had gotten its name because in earlier days, it had stood at a crossroads, and a woman had opened a small store that sold pies to travelers. Store and proprietor had long since gone but the name had persisted. During the early years of the depression, several families of displaced farmers from Oklahoma and Texas had ended up at the parched little town and stayed. They had begun to farm and others had come. By 1940, when the Lees arrived, Pie Town was a small but thriving village, operating on the principle of self-help and community effort. Lee's eye was caught by the way the folks of Pie Town were slowly but surely improving themselves. Newly arrived families lived in dugout houses and sod shacks. Better established families were in the process of moving into better quarters that they had built with the help of neighbors. The late 1930s were good rain years in the area and crops were coming up. There was talk of irrigation. The whole area was reminiscent of the frontier, but here the elapsed time between frontier and farming community was telescoped. Lee could see both phases at once.[39]

The pictures which Lee took of Pie Town appeared in *U. S. Camera* in October, 1941. They created quite a stir. Very few people at that time had considered using a camera to dissect the

Pie Town, New Mexico,
1940. Russell Lee.

At the community sing,
Pie Town, New Mexico,
1940. Russell Lee.

social and economic forces at work in a town, but Lee had proved
that it could be done. The techniques that he pioneered in San
Augustine and Pie Town have yet to be developed fully, but sociologists and anthropologists are beginning to see real possibilities
for the scientific use of cameras along the lines that he mapped
out in 1939 and 1940.[40]

In the course of its development and growth, the historical
section developed many new photographic possibilities. Beginning
as a propaganda agency for a controversial federal project, the
group broadened its interests from rural poverty to include small
towns, cities, and good farms and farm lands. Because its photographers were able to see the social and economic interconnections
between farm, town, and city, the pictures they left were immense-
ly richer than they might have been had the focus been maintained rigorously on rural problems alone.

By 1940 the agency had reached maturity and the legend "FSA
Photograph" had become a commonplace in magazines and books.
Stryker's prestige within the government was high because of his
proven ability to use photographs to illustrate an idea. His staff
was growing larger: new photographers were being added and new
projects were being attempted. Stryker had caught a vision. He
had decided to document America during the decade and he was
doing it. Only the clouds of war threatened his plans.

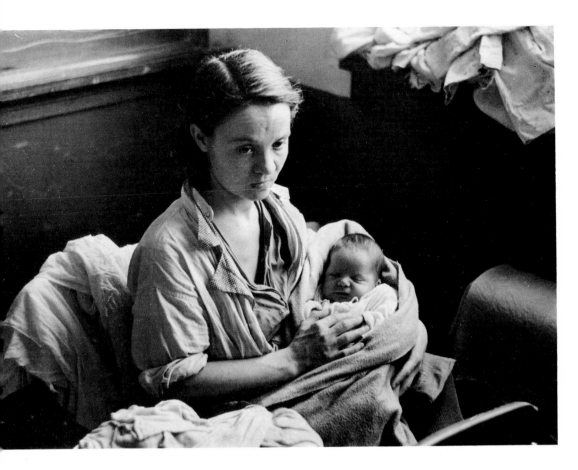

Flood refugees, Missouri,
1937. Russell Lee.

VI

Putting the
Pictures to Work

The Resettlement Administration and the later Farm Security Administration had come into existence because of the problems of rural poverty. Tugwell had created the historical section to help publicize these problems. Therefore in order to justify the appropriations that were being made for its work and for the larger programs of the RA and FSA, the historical section was expected to get its pictures before the public. This could be done in a number of ways.

The agency itself could sponsor publications using the photographs; exhibitions could be planned using historical section pictures; magazine articles and, later, books would reach an even wider audience. One of Stryker's major responsibilities was to see that the photographs his people took received maximum use. As with other facets of the historical section experience, no single set of generalizations will fit the entire seven-year period during which the project functioned. The techniques used in the early days gave way to more sophisticated methods in the later years. As interests changed, emphases also changed. Only one generalization may be said to apply to the entire period: Stryker and his team were effective, both as propagandists and as pioneers of new esthetic styles in photography.

The historical section began to function in the fall of 1935. By early winter in 1936, agency pictures began to appear in magazines that were sympathetic to the aims of the Resettlement Administration. In January, 1936, *Survey Graphic*, the socially conscious publication of the Kellogg family, ran an article on the plight of poor farmers in the South. The article, "Relief and the Sharecropper," by Lillian Davis, was illustrated by two RA photographs by Arthur Rothstein. One, a full-page picture, showed a young boy in ragged clothing standing near a tumbled-down barn with his mother seated nearby. The title was "They's Slim Pickin's" and the general impression was one of unmitigated defeat and disaster. The other photograph, a small one at the end of the article, pictured an old man with his mule. Both pictures were strong visual statements of rural hopelessness and inertia. They supported the plea by the writer for better programs of rural relief.[1]

Survey Graphic was a pioneer in using government photography. The editors had used pictures that Dorothea Lange had made for the state of California for at least a year before the historical section began to function.[2] They had also been utilizing the photographs that Lewis Hine took for the Tennessee Valley Authority.[3] But *Survey Graphic* was somewhat exceptional in this regard. Many magazines and newspapers voiced objections to the use of government-financed photographs. In the early days, these fears revolved around three basic problems. First, there was a general feeling that government photography must necessarily be very slanted or propagandistic in nature; thus, government photographers could not be trusted. Then there was the "free enterprise" thesis that government photographers were moving into areas in competition with publishers who had to show a profit at the end of the year. Finally, there was a submerged problem of jealousy because of the high quality of the historical section's output. Many professional photographers resented the fact that Stryker's photographers could produce work so obviously superior to the run-of-the-mill. Feelings of inadequacy were sometimes translated into antipathy.[4]

Opposition to the work of the historical section might express itself in a magazine's refusal to use RA or, later, FSA pictures. More often the photographs were simply used without proper credit being given to either the agency or the photographer. Such practice was common in the early days, and Stryker fought a constant battle to insure that proper credit lines were given. Evidence of his efforts can be found in many letters. The best, however, is in a letter of his to Dorothea Lange. In this case, she was preparing to turn in a story to *Life*. Stryker wrote:

> I think it would be advisable, if you had the time, to plan the story and the lay-out for *Life*, letting me know whenever it goes forward. . . . The important thing is that I be prepared at this end to scrap with those boys or they will be a little bit ruthless with the pictures. . . . They are apparently very anxious to get this, and I think we can score with them on the credit line both to yourself and to the Resettlement. . . . They are slowly coming around to our views that the credit line is a pretty low cost for good pictures. . . . Once the article is ready, I will be glad to battle with the boys on the 21 floor of the Chrysler Building for credit lines and the maintaining of your lay-out and captions; in fact, I would welcome such a battle.[5]

On the other hand, if a magazine would use his agency's pictures only if it could have them without giving credit, Stryker would usually accept the situation. The basic need was to get the pictures before the public; direct publicity for his own group was a secondary consideration. In 1937, for example, the newly created *Look* used major layouts of FSA photographs at least three different times. These pictures were not credited, yet they are easily recognized today because some of the best known work of the FSA was included.[6]

During 1936 and much of 1937, Stryker had to depend on what might be called "friendly" sources for the main bulk of his publicity. There would always be the Kelloggs at *Survey Graphic.* Camera magazines such as *U.S. Camera* could always be counted on to want to see good pictures. Finally, there were the internal publications of the Resettlement Administration itself. During the first two years, much of Stryker's time was spent providing pictures for agency pamphlets and special reports.

In March, 1936, the first major article on the programs of the Resettlement Administration appeared in *Survey Graphic.* Its author, Edwin W. Embree, had worked with Will Alexander, then assistant administrator of the RA, on the Rosenwald Fund for the development of opportunities for southern Negroes. He was highly sympathetic to the agency's work and the article was definitely friendly in tone. The article, "Southern Farm Tenancy: The Way Out of Its Evils," was illustrated by three RA photographs.[7] Two were by Arthur Rothstein and one was by Ben Shahn. All three appeared in large formats and contributed effectively to the presentation of the story. Tugwell and others who wanted to see the programs of the RA powerfully presented to the American people could hardly fail to be pleased by such an article.

In June, 1936, *Survey Graphic* featured a cover picture by Arthur Rothstein for the RA. Rothstein had gotten a picture of a strong young man in the clothes and straw hat of a farmer, smiling broadly. The picture exuded strength, youth, and health. By contrast, in September of that year, *Survey Graphic* featured a two-page portfolio of Dorothea Lange's pictures of destitute sharecroppers titled "Draggin'-Around People."[8] One of the photographs in this series was the now famous "Migrant Madonna" or "Migrant Mother." The portfolio provided a visual preface to an article by Dorothea Lange's husband, economist Paul Schuster Taylor, titled "From The Ground Up."[9]

Taylor, in this case, concerned himself with the resettlement farms that the RA had created in the West. Farmers who had

Sharecropper family,
Hazelhurst, Georgia,
1937. Dorothea Lange.
Library of Congress

Family bound for Krebs,
Oklahoma, from Idabel,
Oklahoma, 1939. Dorothea Lange.
Library of Congress

not been able to make a living unassisted because of marginal
lands and falling crop prices were resettled on government land
with long-term loans and assistance. They were encouraged to try
different crops and a genuine attempt was made to return them to
effective citizenship. Like everything else about the RA, the program was controversial. Taylor provided an effective defense, and
his wife provided four photographs of rural resettlement projects
in California and New Mexico showing the improved standards
of both farming and living under the new programs.

The sort of defensive propaganda that articles in *Survey Graphic*
supplied was carried over into internal publications of the Resettlement Administration. Among these, two of the earliest (1936) to
make extensive use of effective documentary photographs were
RA pamphlets. One, titled simply *Resettlement Administration,*
presented a general statement of agency programs and aims. The
other was a more specialized document on land use, titled *America's Land.* Both attempted to explain complex government programs in the simplest and most understandable terms. Both also
made extensive use of historical section photographs. These pictures and their captions could make a point about soil erosion
or substandard rural housing that could not be made with equal
impact in any other way. No paragraph about farm tenancy and
its evils could quite capture the forcefulness of a photograph of
a slack-jawed woman in front of a worn-out field. Both publications were designed for wide distribution to farmers and others
interested in rural programs. They were small enough to fit into
the hip pocket of a pair of overalls. The pictures were spaced so
as to sustain the interest of men who read little. Almost every
page in both pamphlets carried at least one photograph.

The small pamphlets such as *Resettlement Administration* and
America's Land were designed to make the RA's programs understandable to those who most desperately needed to know about
them. The articles in *Survey Graphic* were a way of reaching
the public at large. One important group remained. The United
States Congress, holder of the national purse strings, could not
be ignored. In order to meet the need for a comprehensive statement of the programs and responsibilities of the Resettlement
Administration, a publication titled *First Annual Report of the
Resettlement Administration* was prepared in November, 1936.
In 173 pages the report gave a complete account of the organization of the agency, its divisions, and its programs.[10]

As in other publications of the RA, photographs were used
extensively and effectively in the *First Annual Report.* Unfortu-

Southern West Virginia,
1938. Marion Post
Wolcott.

nately, individual photographers were not identified in the captions, but one familiar with each cameraman's individualistic style can recognize the work of Rothstein, Lange, Mydans, Evans, and even Shahn. Almost fifty photographs were used to illustrate the report; and almost all would stand as effective statements today. It was an impressive performance for a group that, in those early days, had no clear idea about what it was supposed to be doing. Stryker and his team might not have had a very definite concept of their function in 1936, but they were obviously successful propagandists for the agency's cause.

During the first two years that Stryker headed the historical section, he was involved a great deal with what might fairly be described as propaganda. That is, much of his work was aimed at direct justification of RA programs in terms of specific agricultural problems. "We need better programs to use soil so that *this* woman may have a better life." To describe Stryker as simply a propagandist, however, would be a distortion of the facts. As early as mid-1936, there is evidence that he was interested in pictures that could stand on their own merits and meet the critical inspection of the photographic world.

In the late summer of 1936, *U.S. Camera* began to plan its annual exhibition. In 1935 and again in 1936, the magazine had sponsored a large salon showing of outstanding prints and then had published these in an annual. It was considered a major achievement to be represented in this particular show. The exhibition and annual for 1936 included four photographs by historical section photographers. Dorothea Lange was invited to send her photograph "Migrant Mother" and Arthur Rothstein was represented by the now famous skull photographs and two other pictures.[11] It was the first time that the historical section had been represented in a "serious" collection of prints. Stryker and the others quickly decided to pursue this field more actively in the future. When the College Art Association asked Stryker for a traveling exhibit of agency pictures in October, 1936, he responded with 110 prints mounted and ready to ship.[12]

Shows such as the *U.S. Camera* Salon were always trying experiences for Dorothea Lange. She took them very seriously and insisted on having her negatives shipped back to her so that she could make her own prints and sign them. When Edwin Locke, Stryker's assistant during 1936 and part of 1937, suggested that the prints be made in Washington in order to save time and money, she was adamant! "Please mister, that idea is no good. This show is the most important photographic show we have. It tours

Store window, Bethlehem,
Pennsylvania, 1935.
Walker Evans.

the country. It tours Europe. I couldn't afford to show prints, unsigned, which I have not even *seen*. I'll send the negatives right back."[13]

Lange's insistence on complete control was unusual. Most of the photographers preferred to have the laboratory in Washington take care of the technical matters of making prints. Often their trust of the Washington staff went considerably further. When the Carl Zeiss company asked for a representative set of Resettlement Administration pictures in early 1937, Arthur Rothstein simply wrote to Stryker suggesting several negatives that he thought would make good prints and left the rest to Stryker's discretion. In the case of Russell Lee, the element of trust reached a peak. Lee was still on the road when the request from Zeiss came in. He had not yet seen any of his own work nor would he be able to for some time. In this case he simply gave carte blanche to Stryker. "By all means, go ahead with the selection of the pictures for the Zeiss exhibit. I am sure that you, Arthur, and Walker Evans can make a fine choice of not only the pictures but also of arrangements for the layout."[14]

This sort of amiability and trust may be one reason that Stryker kept Rothstein and Lee on the payroll through every storm of financial panic when others were laid off or terminated.

Exhibits such as those planned for *U.S. Camera* and Carl Zeiss had little direct impact on legislation because legislators seldom went to see them. They had little impact on farmers either, for the same reason. On the other hand, it was through these early exhibitions that Stryker's team began to make a name for itself as the most exciting group of photographers in the country. By enlarging their reputation with other photographers and magazine publishers, the historical section cameramen were able to gain acceptance for their work in magazines and other publications from which government photographers would normally have been barred. By continuing to fight for full credit lines, naming the photographer and the agency, Stryker made sure that anyone who was interested could determine the source of these hard-hitting documentary photographs. Any magazine or other publication that wanted to use RA or FSA prints was welcome to do so, so long as credit was given and the factual captions were not distorted. In this way the exhibitions were used as stepping stones to greater exposure in national publications.

Exhibitions of strong photographs of rural poverty could have a definite impact on the thinking of urban people. In cities such as Boston, New York, and Los Angeles, a small but influential

Sons of a fisherman,
Olga, Louisiana, 1938.
Russell Lee.

segment of the population attended shows and reacted to the photographs. In many instances these viewers had never been confronted with the problems of rural distress, and the photographs were their first contact with sharecroppers and "Okies." No better example of the power of documentary photographs could be found than that provided by the International Photographic Exhibition held at Grand Central Palace in New York City in the spring of 1938.

Willard Morgan, who sponsored the great exhibit, had spent most of his adult life promoting good photography. In 1930 he had become the United States representative for the then very new Leica camera. In 1932 he had begun the excellent magazine *Leica Photography*, devoted to publishing the best in small-camera photography.[15] In early 1938 he contacted Roy Stryker with his plan to produce a truly international exhibit of great photographs. It was to be the most elaborate show that New York had ever seen and Morgan wanted the historical section to be a major contributor.[16]

During the spring of that year, both Arthur Rothstein and Russell Lee were kept in Washington as much as possible. Their job was to select and supervise the printing of the pictures that would go to the Grand Central show. They puzzled over hundreds of possible photographs: they tried various combinations and sizes. In the end they decided on about seventy prints, enlarged somewhat more than usual. They ranged in size from 11" × 14" to 30" × 40". Included were many of the finest pictures in the file.[17]

The show opened in April and was a success from the beginning. The FSA panels were particularly well received. In a letter to his friend and one-time assistant Ed Locke, Roy could not resist the chance to gloat a little. "Our part of the show went across in a big way," he wrote. "Arthur and Russell did a grand job of hanging those pictures. It is not exaggerating a bit to say that we scooped the show. Even Steichen went to the show in a perfunctory manner and got a surprise when he ran into our section."[18] For Stryker, who was so passionately interested in photography as a tool for social documentation, applause from Edward Steichen, dean of serious, "artistic" photographers, was a sweet victory indeed. It proved that his group was making pictures that could stand on their own merits as fine images as well as documents.

Steichen was not alone in his recognition of the high quality of FSA photography. Elizabeth McCausland, art critic for the Springfield, Massachusetts, *Sunday Union and Republican* and one of the most respected thinkers in the field of art and photog-

Mrs. Mary Willis, widow
with two children, on
rented farm near Wood-
ville, Greene County,
Georgia, 1941. Jack
Delano.

raphy, thought the FSA section of the show was one of the best she had ever seen.

> After the usual diet of the art world—cream puffs, eclairs, and such—the hard, bitter reality of these photographs is the tonic the soul needs. They are like a sharp wind, sweeping away the weariness, the fever and the fret of life. For so grim is the truth they present that the vapors of pseudo-intellectual culture are immediately dispelled. In them we see the faces of the American people. The American people which lives under the threat of unemployment, hunger and eviction. We see the farmers, the sharecroppers, the homeless migrant agricultural workers, the children who suffer from malnutrition, the whole families whose homes are part of that dreadful substandard "one-third of a nation."
>
> In these photographs we might see also (if we were completely honest and fearless intellectually) the faces of ourselves. For, if the past decade has taught us no other thing, it has showed that the vaunted economic security of the prosperous citizen is no more secure than the marginal life of the depressed millions.[19]

If Stryker and his people needed more proof that the art world was beginning to take them seriously, it was on the way. Within weeks the New York Museum of Modern Art had offered to take the entire FSA exhibit from the Grand Central show on the road throughout the United States.[20] Stryker was only too happy to have his section's work under the sponsorship of the respected museum. That same summer it was announced that the museum was producing a major exhibition of Walker Evans' work, done during the FSA years. It was to be called *American Photographs* and was the first time that the museum had ever sponsored a one-man show for a photographer. The exhibit would also be published in book form.[21]

If the praise from top artists and critics was pleasing, equally interesting were the comments made by ordinary people who came to see the Grand Central Exhibition. The pictures had evidently gripped the attention of passers-by as well as trained observers. While the show was being hung, Arthur Rothstein had gotten an idea. Why not put some cards out on a table so that people could write down their immediate reactions to the pictures?[22] This had been done and the results had surpassed everybody's expectations. The comments had ranged from a simple and direct "It stinks!" to "Marvelous documentary photographs." "More of this kind of thing might awaken people really to do something to alleviate the suffering."[23] A majority registered shock, but were strongly impressed with the photographs and the rural poverty that they showed. Almost 500 people took the time to register

Coal miner's child taking
home kerosene for lamps.
Company houses and coal
tipple in background,
Pursglove, West Virginia,
undated. Marion Post
Wolcott.

their comments and almost all were favorable. There were few neutral reactions. Whatever else it might have accomplished, the Grand Central show had awakened people.

In the wake of the exhibition, the FSA began to receive more and more calls for its photographs. *U.S. Camera* decided to feature the photographs from the Grand Central show in their 1938 annual. The FSA was given thirty-two pages of the annual that year and an excellent layout.[24] It was wonderful national exposure. Thousands read *U.S. Camera* who would never have a chance to see the photographs hanging on a wall. It was also good for Stryker's prestige within the government organization. When it became time to discuss budgets in late 1938, the upper echelons of the FSA could be expected to remember the national publicity that Stryker's group had gotten for their programs, and it was hoped they would act accordingly. After the article appeared, Roy wrote to Dorothea Lange to give her the latest gossip: "U.S. Camera has done no end of good here. Baldwin and Alexander and the whole group of assistants have been much impressed. We got copies for Dr. Will to give to the Secretary and his staff. I have bought several copies of them and have been giving them out to various people where I thought it would do the most good. I am astounded more and more as the days go by at the number of people who have been impressed by this job."[25]

The work within the FSA would, of course, continue. In 1937 the historical section illustrated an agency pamphlet titled *Farm Tenancy—The Remedy: Twenty Questions Asked and Answered.* The object of this small publication was to advocate the passage of the Bankhead-Jones Act. There would also be pamphlets on Greenbelt towns and other subjects of importance to agricultural programs. By 1938, however, much of the best publicity for farm problems and farming in general was coming from the outside, through commercial use of FSA photographs. One of the most successful areas of commercial exploitation was that of the picture book.

The idea of a picture book was not new in 1938, but the interest shown by commercial publishing houses was a new phenomenon. Stryker had been interested in the use of pictures in books since the Columbia University days when he, Tugwell, and Monroe had worked on *American Economic Life.* The idea had never been completely dropped, but it had been eclipsed for a time. In 1936 Stryker and several of the photographers had worked with Rupert B. Vance, a sociologist from the University of North Carolina, to bring out a short book titled *How the Other Half is*

Housed.[26] It was not a sophisticated work. A few pages of type, explaining southern rural housing problems in simple terms; twenty pages of photographs laid out two to a page; and a short statement about the agency that had brought out the book, the Southern Policy Committee; and the book was finished. Designed to sell for fifteen cents, it was almost a pamphlet, yet it was an attempt to put words and pictures together to make a point, and it was done by an outside agency making use of RA photographs.

The first really successful combination of words and pictures in book form to tell about rural poverty was not the production of the historical section. Margaret Bourke-White and her husband, Erskine Caldwell, had become aware of the fine work that Stryker and his photographers were doing through articles in *Survey Graphic* and exhibits. Bourke-White, already a successful commercial photographer on the staff of *Life,* saw possibilities in the idea of a book of words and pictures about poverty in the South. In early 1937 *You Have Seen Their Faces* appeared in bookstores.[27]

You Have Seen Their Faces was in some ways a beautiful book. The photographs were large, well displayed, and beautifully printed. The writing aspired to objectivity. On a deeper level, however, the book was exploitative. The photographs, and the writing as well, often descended to levels of taste that would have been foreign to FSA photographers. Physical deformities of photographic subjects were somtimes played upon. Caldwell too often dwelt on sordid details of lynchings and other wretched aspects of Negro-white relations. There was no attempt to postulate programs for change. Unlike the FSA photographers, Caldwell and Bourke-White remained essentially Olympian, observers of problems yet rather unconcerned about the possibilities of reform. The photographs and the dramatic writings were merely presented and the reader was left to draw his own conclusions.

The book was not perfect; few are. But it was a commercial and, to a certain extent, a critical success. Because of its sales records, other publishers were attracted to the idea of doing books on rural poverty. This opened rich opportunities to the historical section. More often than not, publishers preferred to use photographs taken by the agency in preference to sending a commercial photographer into the field. By 1937 the picture file in Washington was quite full and the photographs could be used without charge; thus, the editors came to Stryker.

Shortly after the appearance of Bourke-White and Caldwell's book, Archibald MacLeish had an idea. Why not do a book of

poetry on depression problems and illustrate it with photographs?
He contacted C. A. Pierce at Harcourt, Brace and Company in
New York and sold the idea to him. Through the publishing company, Stryker was brought into the project.[28] He was receptive
to the proposition and that summer MacLeish came to Washington
to look through the file of photographs. The collection of pictures
he found there had a tremendous impact on the poet. So strong
were they that his entire conception of the project changed. He
had planned to write a poem that could be illustrated with pictures. Now, he decided to pick out photographs that could be
illustrated by a poem.[29] The result was a searchingly honest small
book, which he titled, with heavy irony, *Land of the Free.* The
message of this work might be summed up in the phrase "We
wonder." The photographs and MacLeish's words told of thousands of harassed men and women for whom the old formulae
were not working. "We don't know," he wrote.

> We wonder if the liberty is done:
> The dreaming is finished
> We can't say
> We aren't sure
> Or if there's something different
> men can dream
> Or if there's something different
> men can mean by
> Liberty. . . .
> We wonder
> We don't know
> We're asking[30]

Like Caldwell and Bourke-White, MacLeish was not in a position
to propose a complete investigation of rural problems, nor was
he prepared to offer concrete solutions. But he could offer honest
questions and a photographic coverage that was national in scope.
The photographs in *Land of the Free* were so strong that they
sometimes overshadowed the text, but the overall effect was quite
successful from the standpoint of both art and propaganda. No one
who read *Land of the Free* could fail to grasp its message that the
country folk were restless and in need of stabilizing programs.

After *Land of the Free,* books making use of FSA photographs
proliferated. In 1938 Herman C. Nixon brought out a short but
extremely well-done study of tenancy in the South, titled *Forty
Acres and Steel Mules,* which was lavishly illustrated with the
agency's photographs.[31] Walker Evans' *American Photographs*
also appeared in 1938, published by the Museum of Modern Art
in New York. *American Photographs* was a solid critical success,

Wife of unemployed
miner, with tuberculosis,
Marine, West Virginia,
1938. Marion Post
Wolcott.

but it probably accomplished little in the way of publicizing rural problems. Only thirty-five of nearly eighty photographs in the book were done under the auspices of the historical section. Many of them were strong statements but they were published without captions, which somewhat limited their value.

One of the strongest statements of rural relief and rehabilitation came from a novelist who knew nothing about photography and used no photographs in his work. In 1938 a young man named John Steinbeck came into the FSA offices and told the clerks that he wanted to do a book on migrant labor. C. B. Baldwin, then assistant administrator under Will Alexander, referred him to Roy Stryker, who spent several days showing him the file of pictures. After the time in the historical section, Steinbeck was allowed to go into the field in the company of an FSA official, both men disguised as migrant workers. With his observations in the files of the historical section and his experiences in the field as a basis, Steinbeck produced *The Grapes of Wrath.* The book first appeared in March, 1939, and was immediately a tremendous success. Later it was the source for a movie by the same title. The powerful influence of the photo file can be felt throughout the book and is quite obvious in the movie. C. B. Baldwin remembered the movie as a high point in effective propaganda for the FSA.[32]

In 1939 Dorothea Lange and her husband, Paul Taylor, brought out a small but beautifully executed book titled *American Exodus.*[33] Here was as concise a statement of the basic problems that rural America faced as would ever be put on paper. A blending of words and pictures that gets across a body of information, *American Exodus* had a power and charm that is still evident today. It marked a kind of apogee for FSA illustrated books. After *American Exodus* books illustrated by the historical section would begin to reflect their growing involvement in the larger aspects of American life: the successful farmer, the small town, and the city. *American Exodus* was one of the last great "problem books" from this period. There never was a better one.

Lange and Taylor saw as a major problem the fact that farmers could not make a living on lands they had worked for years and therefore had taken to the road. The theme of *American Exodus* was farm families on the move. Every major agricultural section of the country was visited and photographed. The tragedy was clear. Americans were moving West, but there was nothing for them to do when they got there. Starvation wages in the Nipomo pea fields, life in tents and shacks, rags and bitterness were all

Washington, D.C., 1941.
Marion Post Wolcott.

that the displaced could look forward to. Small government sub-
sidies could give short-term aid, but they could not change the
basic problem.

Combined with Lange's powerful photographs were the strong
and carefully reasoned words of Paul Taylor. Lange spoke from
the heart. Taylor probed with his mind. What were the factors
causing rural problems? Loss of foreign markets? The tractor?
Overproduction? What programs could the government utilize
to bring about an end to this rural disaster? Taylor examined
each section of the country and reached some general conclusions.
They did not even agree with some of the programs of the FSA,
but they were honest and history has treated them well.

> It is plain that with advances in agricultural techniques, the country
> requires fewer farmers rather than more. Probably nine-tenths of
> the commercial production of agriculture at this time is supplied by
> well under half of the nation's farms. Mechanization accentuates this.
> Further, the income of agriculture is not great enough to support
> more people adequately. The advance of the machine should not, and
> probably cannot be halted. . . . The real opportunity for large-scale
> absorption of the displaced must lie in the direction of industrial ex-
> pansion, not in crowding them back on the land where already they
> are surplus.[34]

American Exodus was published by a small press and never
received the national attention that it deserved. But it did form
a fitting climax to Dorothea Lange's career with the historical
section. It was her finest work prior to her retrospective exhibition at the Museum of Modern Art in 1965. Unfortunately, it was
her last work for the historical section.

During the writing of *American Exodus,* friction developed
between Stryker and Lange. The photographer, as always, deeply
concerned about quality, had insisted on making all prints herself. Stryker had objected to this practice and the time it took
from other, more pressing matters. Finally, however, the precious
negatives had been duly boxed up and sent to California. While
she had the negatives in her possession, Lange had taken the
liberty of having several of them retouched. One in particular
was a source of trouble. Lange's great "Migrant Mother" photograph had always bothered her a little. Just at the instant that
she had taken the picture, a hand had reached out to draw the
tent flap back a bit further and the photograph had caught a dis-
embodied thumb in the foreground. That thumb had worried
Lange. So, when she prepared the picture for *American Exodus,*
the thumb was retouched out of the negative.

This was a simple technique that she had employed hundreds
of times during her career as a portrait photographer. For Stryker

it was a serious lapse of taste. He was quite bitter over the incident. As a series of letters passed between the two on the subject, the rift widened.[35] Later, when he saw the finished book, Stryker would concede that it was "a swell job."[36] But Lange went off of the FSA payroll permanently in 1940.[37] Ironically, "Migrant Mother" did not appear in the final version of *American Exodus*.

By 1940 the historical section was a seasoned agency, prepared to use a wide variety of techniques to place the need for farm security before the nation. An increasing number of articles employed its photographs as illustrative material. As the section broadened its interests, it also broadened the possibilities for use of its pictures. In 1940 and 1941 many kinds of books appeared which used FSA pictures. Sherwood Anderson's *Home Town* was a success in 1941. That same year James Agee and Walker Evans finally succeeded in bringing out *Let Us Now Praise Famous Men*. It was a great work of art but its timing was poor. People were more and more caught up in the coming of war and had little interest in rural poverty as it had existed in the South five years earlier. The book's sales were minuscule.

More successful were books that related to the problems of the post-1940 world. Richard Wright's *Twelve Million Black Voices*, in which Edwin Rosskam collaborated in 1941, was a fine blending of words and pictures, and the problem that Wright investigated was relevant. He was interested in the migration of southern blacks to the North. Why did they leave? What happened to them when they arrived in the North? Was there any place for the Negro in American culture? Certainly the Negro had been a major concern of the FSA programs in the South, and it was logical for the agency to follow his progress in the North. The book was extremely well done and had a large sale.

It was also in 1941 that the University of North Carolina Press brought out a complete study of southern tenant farming, which was illustrated by FSA pictures. *Sharecroppers All* by Arthur Raper was an excellent sociological and economic study of sharecropping and its effects upon the South.[38] Included were thirty-five photographs from the agency's files. The best efforts of the historical section were there. Lange, Lee, Mydans, Shahn, Post, and Rothstein all were represented.

In addition to work on books, the historical section continued to use exhibitions and articles to help urban America understand rural America. Russell Lee's fine articles on San Augustine, Texas, and Pie Town, New Mexico, were highly evocative of disappearing patterns of small-town and farm life.[39] *Survey Graphic* occasionally included articles on farm problems or government pro-

grams to alleviate rural distress.[40] Exhibits continued to go out
from the photographic laboratory of the historical section. In
fact the exhibitions became rather sophisticated affairs.

After Edwin Rosskam joined the historical section in 1938, a
large part of his time was devoted to designing traveling exhibits
and slide shows. Some of these were of a general nature, emphasizing the artistic photography of the FSA cameramen; others
were essentially teaching devices related to specific agency programs. This latter type of show was in demand at county fairs
and other rural gatherings. FSA photographs were a favorite propaganda weapon of regional agency personnel. By 1940 the direc-
tors of the various regional programs, well aware that a picture
was worth a thousand words, were clamoring for exhibits. Rosskam and Stryker put together a series of traveling shows that
were kept on the road much of the time. These usually consisted
of about twenty 11″ × 14″ prints mounted on 15″ × 20″ white
mat boards.[41] On some occasions the entire show was planned,
complete with captions, and sent around permanently mounted
on large panels.

Because each region had quite different problems and ideol-
ogies, sending a prepackaged show from the Washington office
could sometimes lead to problems. When Rosskam sent a show to
West Texas in early 1940, a nervous and race-conscious regional
director was quick to criticize what he considered to be a breach
of the "Southern code of ethics."

> Why was it necessary for Mr. Rosskam to use a picture of a Negro
> farmer on the fourth panel? Surely he had photographs of German
> farmers, Russian farmers, Italian farmers, Irish farmers, etc. Yet he,
> for some reason I cannot calculate, used a Negro farmer.
> I believe I am sincerely sympathetic to all races, including Negroes.
> . . . Yet the photographs of Negroes to be used in Region 12 are quite
> objectionable.
> I do not wish to appear as a bull in a china shop, but knowing the
> people in this region as I do, I doubt the wisdom of using a panel show-
> ing a Negro farmer beside a panel showing a white farm woman. . . .
> Even a Spanish-American farmer's picture would not be popular in
> West Texas.[42]

Such complaints, however, were rare. Generally regional officials were happy to get any visual material that the national office
could supply. In fact they often wanted more photographs of their
own local projects than the historical section could provide. This
was particularly true of the California area. Dorothea Lange, who
lived in region 9 (the far West), felt this problem keenly and often
pressured Stryker for extra prints. One of the last exchanges of
letters between the two concerned her conviction that region 9

Entrance to house in
Negro section of Chicago,
1941. Russell Lee.

Chicago, Illinois, 1941.
Russell Lee.

was not being adequately covered and the regional office was not getting enough prints.[43] Actually, of course, the laboratory in Washington was working at maximum output during all of the later years trying to meet the demands.

By 1940 the group which had been responsible for so many changes in the field of photography and journalism was becoming the subject of journalism itself. Articles began to appear dealing with Roy Stryker and the tremendously effective team which he had created. Stories of this type were of course quite flattering, but they also served the purpose of further publicizing the agency and its programs. It was impossible to write about the photographers and their pictures without discussing the agency for which they worked.

The first article to appear (and in some ways, one of the best) was by Hartley E. Howe, son of Franklin Roosevelt's close friend Louis Howe. "You Have Seen Their Pictures" appeared in the April, 1940, *Survey Graphic*.[44] Howe gave a brief description of the section, the reasons that had brought it into existence, and the directions it had taken. He described Stryker and the new methods that his project had developed to use government photographs. Finally, Howe defended the need for a government photographic agency.

> There undoubtedly are points in the FSA photographic program open to legitimate dispute. How far, for example, should a government agency go in using publicity—whether pictures or text—to further its own policies? A line must be drawn somewhere between no publicity at all—which would make those in office unable to show the public what they have been doing and why—and the propaganda of a totalitarian state. It seems as if government sponsored publicity which is accurate, and which tells about policies and problems rather than individuals and parties, is not only harmless but desirable. Certainly FSA photographs come well within this category.[45]

Soon after the appearance of Howe's article, others appeared, mostly in magazines devoted to photography. As the documentary photograph caught the imagination of photographers all over the country, there developed a genuine interest in the men and women who had brought the new style into popularity. In 1941 *Popular Photography* carried a major article on Stryker and his accomplishments.[46] The high point of this interest, however, came and went in 1941. By 1942 the national attention was riveted on events in Europe and the coming of war to the United States. As the nation girded for war, Stryker and his staff would find their situation changing also, not always in ways that boded well for the future of the historical section.

VII

1941–1943:
The Impact of War

By 1941 the historical section of the Farm Security Administration
had amply justified its existence to those who were at all willing
to admit its validity. Its photographs were appearing in almost
all of the major magazines, as well as in books, pamphlets, traveling exhibits, and museums. The central office in Washington
was comfortable. The new facilities in the Auditor's Building, at
14th Street and Independence Avenue, were roomy and air conditioned, a far cry from the earlier days when a few square yards
of borrowed floor space from the Department of Agriculture had
served the purpose. The staff was larger and systems and techniques were more settled. In short the Stryker group had, at least
tentatively, entered the "establishment." But, at the very peak of
their success, forces were at work which would undermine the
unit. Within two and a half years, the group would cease to exist.

For Stryker the early forties were good years. His staff was
competent and growing. When Arthur Rothstein left in 1940 to
take a job with *Look,* Stryker was able to find an excellent replacement in Jack Delano.[1] About the same time he began utilizing
John Vachon as a photographer, moving him gradually into the
work from the position of trainee and clerk in charge of the photographic file. Stryker's staff in Washington was experienced and
competent. His personal secretary, young and personable Clara
Dean "Toots" Wakeham, was a pillar of strength to the entire
team. Often she wrote and answered letters to the photographers
in Stryker's name, so complete was her knowledge of the department. The darkroom, under the supervision of Roy Dixon, was
as modern as any in the country. With it the section could turn
out anything needed from standard 8″ × 10″ pictures to huge
murals, and the work could be done quickly. In 1941 another
photographer, John Collier, Jr., joined the staff, and a young black
man, Gordon Parks, was taken into the agency as a trainee. If

ever an agency seemed well established, the historical section qualified.

The new men extended the range of interests and abilities available to Stryker. Collier and Delano were both professionals in the best sense of the word. Delano's interest in photography had developed while he was a student at the Pennsylvania Academy of Fine Arts in Philadelphia. His photographs of Pennsylvania and New York City were so perceptive that the academy sent him to Europe to continue his studies. He officially joined the FSA staff on May 6, 1940.[2] Stryker remembered him as a deeply sensitive person who had a knack for summing up a great deal in one picture. "Russell [Lee] was the taxonomist. . . . He takes apart and gives you all the details of the plant. He lays it on the table and says 'There you are, Sir, in all its parts. . . .' Jack [Delano] was the artist, and being an artist would say, 'What one picture could I take that would say Vermont?' "[3]

On Delano's first trip for the FSA he was sent into New England. This was becoming almost a standard first assignment. Stryker loved the area and knew it well. In fact the chief of the historical section had even purchased a small recreational farm in the area for himself and his family. One of the best ways to test a photographer's mettle was to send him North to "do New England." In September, 1940, Jack and his wife, Irene, set out to photograph the rural Northeast in the fall. Stryker's instructions were explicit and humorous:

> Please watch for "Autumn" pictures, as calls are beginning to come in for them and we are short. These should be rather the symbol of Autumn, particularly in the Northeast—cornfields, pumpkins, raking leaves, roadside stands with fruits of the land. Emphasize the idea of abundance—the "horn of plenty" and pour maple syrup over it—you know; mix well with white clouds and put on a sky-blue platter. I know your damned photographer's soul writhes, but to hell with it. Do you think I give a damn about a photographer's soul with Hitler at our doorstep? You are nothing but camera fodder to me.[4]

The trip north was a long one. Jack and Irene were on the road from September through January. Jack photographed the potato harvest in Maine, small towns, commercial chicken raising ("Who the hell can get excited about a chicken?"), and even some defense industries.[5] Delano's pictures of the Pratt and Whitney aircraft works in Norwich, Connecticut, marked a new departure for the historical section. It took some talking and some waiting in outer offices, but Delano did get into the plant and began what would become a major part of the FSA record—the photographs of war industries.[6]

In a Negro home, Heard County, Georgia,
1941. Jack Delano.

Sea town, Stonington, Connecticut, 1940.
Jack Delano. *Library of Congress*

The next spring Jack and Irene were on the road again. This time they headed South. It was the first trip into the southern area for both and they were fascinated. They loved the area. Only the racial attitudes grated. During May and June, most of their time was spent in Green County, Georgia. There the sociologist Arthur Raper was completing his third major study of farm tenancy in the South. The book, *Tenants of the Almighty,* told a hopeful story of better conditions and more stable population since the advent of government programs. The photographs that Delano took captured the feeling of happiness and industry in the formerly poverty-stricken area.[7]

Their work with Raper was pleasant, as the photographs show. But more and more, the historical section photographers were finding themselves recording the ominous story of a nation preparing itself for war. While Delano was still photographing the happy faces and well-kept farms of Green County, a letter from Roy indicated that the agency was taking new directions. He wanted Jack to take a few days off and go over to Fort Benning to photograph the soldiers, showing especially the effect of the military buildup on the surrounding area.

> Soldiers on the street corners, soldiers playing pin ball machines, soldiers playing those little machine guns (target practice).
> I am very anxious that we get additional pictures of the soldiers' life around the towns near big encampments. You can emphasize the congestion in the town and the blocking up of normal facilities caused by the soldiers coming into towns for the weekends. . . . You should by all means try your hand at Phoenix City. Most of the prostitution is on that side of the river. . . . Try to get a picture of a soldier, lonely, trying to pick up a date.[8]

And thus, more and more, it was to be the war that dominated the pictures of the historical section. This was natural, because the war was beginning to dominate the thinking of all Americans, even though the nation was not yet directly involved. As usual the Stryker mind saw through the surface realities and saw the possibilities of a grand-scale essay. The actual fighting would never be within his sphere of interests, but he could cover the home front. Instead of the usual slick pictures of war industries at work, he would send his people out to look beyond, to the effects of the war on the civilian population. What had been a record of a nation fighting depression would become an even greater record of a nation at war with totalitarianism.

In order to tell the story the way he wanted it told, Roy felt that more photographers were needed. Accordingly, in September, 1941, John Collier, Jr., joined the staff.[9] Collier's first assignment

Pittsburgh, Pennsylvania,
1941. Jack Delano.

indicated the change that had taken place in the direction of the historical section. He was sent to Connecticut to photograph in the same plant of Pratt and Whitney aircraft company that Jack Delano had visited the year before. In 1940, when Delano had visited the plant, the trip had been a diversion from the routine of rural photography. In September, 1941, Collier's visit to the factory was in deadly earnest. Now the main story concerned the defense industry, while any work on rural problems would have to be rather incidental. Collier spent weeks in the Pratt and Whitney plant but did find time for trips into the country as well.[10] There he stumbled onto a situation that he could only report. It was the sort of thing that Stryker wanted to know about, the effects of the buildup for war on the people and the land. Near Westport, Connecticut, Collier noticed that most of the land was being bought up by very wealthy people. This move to the soil Collier interpreted as an unconscious effort to escape the pressures of war. "I can get you good coverage," he wrote, "on the rich New Yorker who in terror of the war has taken to the soil, as it were." "Blooded sows, hounds, arabian polo ponies and what have you, all in the eye of answering the old 'living off the soil' gag. All this means that the older farm families which have been hoeing around the rocks since the English burned Danbury are moving out and going to no one knows where."[11]

It would have made a good, tight picture essay of the type that Stryker liked to see, but there was no time. John's pictures of the defense industry were too badly needed, so back he went to Pratt and Whitney, complaining that it was almost impossible to get pictures of typical workers because "typical" workers ("strong and grim") did not exist at Pratt and Whitney. "Many are kids or nice looking old men with white hair, but we shall see."[12]

When he had time for it, John Collier's writing was almost as good as his photography. His poetic soul poured itself out in long letters of observations on people and land. After one short excursion into rural New England, he sent Roy a matchless description of a roadside stand doing a full business and of the intermixing of cultures that was taking place there.

> One of the roadside markets was enormous. Its proprietors were an Italian family who en-masse waited on the host of canny New Englanders who insisted on peeling back each ear of corn before buying it. The general-in-chief, (a portly lady with huge breasts and very large earrings) confided to me that the family was from Genoa, and, that in itself not convincing enough, confided a second time, "We are also half Jewish," and she snapped her chub fingers at the Connecticut yankees—It was wonderful! The family raced up and down between

Ephrata, Pennsylvania. John Collier.

Tobacco sheds, Green-
field, Connecticut, 1941.
John Collier.
Library of Congress

the baskets, crates and piles of every conceivable vegetable and fruit grown in New England, screaming tempting prices, waving huge mossy-green melons at the passers by, biting savagely into red apples and holding forth the undevoured half as sample of their goodness. Needless to say, they were making money. Even the New Englanders couldn't resist this passionate observance of the harvest.[13]

Collier made a fine set of pictures in the best FSA tradition that day, but such experiences were becoming increasingly rare. More normal would be the story that he covered in October, 1941. With winter settling over the Northeast, he became interested in the transportation industry and its relation to the war buildup. In the upper Hudson River Valley, he made the acquaintance of a barge captain and wrote a vivid description of his experience in another letter to Stryker:

> The day broke bitterly cold with a screeching north wind that made me generalize in a dozen ways upon what a sorry day it was for taking pictures. In this state of mind I cruised down to the left side of the river, following the course of the old canal. . . . Schenectady was just around the bend and in the lee of the barge terminal. At least one old tow had tied up for shelter. She was an old-time scow with a neat little cabin aft with a smudge of stove smoke blowing off on the wind. I promptly forgot about the weather and, cramming holders in my pockets, stepped out to take pictures. Woof, the wind damned near ripped the bellows out of my camera and I shivered enough to blur a two-hundredth of a second exposure. Enough was enough, I hailed the barge. "Could I come aboard?" A bushy head wagged out of the hatch and I clambered aboard.[14]

Collier had begun to develop a story on barge traffic and in that letter even went so far as to request Stryker's permission to travel with the barge for a while and shoot a complete story on its activities. Permission arrived too late and the bargeman had shoved off, but Collier did spend several days covering river traffic. The pictures had a bleak, wintry look that gave them impact and emphasized the importance of the water transportation industry. In the earlier days of the FSA the utility of such a story might have been questionable. Given the changed situation, however, it was a perfectly logical choice.

John Vachon, who was to become one of this country's most sensitive photographers, was an unusual product of the historical section. He had come to the agency in the summer of 1936 with little or no interest in photography, a fresh kid with a new-minted college degree from Catholic University and no job. The historical section needed a general helper to run errands and write captions on the backs of photographs. It was not much of a job, but times were hard and Vachon took it. "Well, within a few months I got

Grandfather Romero,
Trampas, New Mexico,
1943. John Collier.

interested in the pictures themselves, and began to know one photographer's work from another, and admire certain pictures. It was in the spring of the next year, '37, when I asked Stryker if I could use a camera just to see what I could do with it, which I had never in my life done or wanted to do. So I borrowed a camera and took pictures around Washington for most of that summer, you know, on my own."[15]

For several years Vachon remained on the Washington staff where he became the primary custodian of the growing file of pictures. It was an important and necessary job, but John wanted more. Every year Stryker would allow him to take a few assignments in areas near Washington, but he was not officially classified as a photographer until 1941. In the early days, while still in the process of seeking a style of his own, Vachon was tremendously influenced by the work of Walker Evans. "I went around looking for Walker Evans' pictures," he recalls. "I remember once in Atlanta where I knew so well a certain house he had photographed. I walked all over town looking for it, and when I had found the real thing, . . . it was like a historic find."[16] In 1941, however, Vachon was sent to the West. When he reached Nebraska, he was in territory that had never been covered by Evans. Here his own style could begin to assert itself, and assert itself it did. His pictures captured the loneliness of the plains with a stark beauty that was both gripping and real.[17]

The case of Gordon Parks was special. The young black photographer was never actually on the payroll of the Farm Security Administration, yet for several months he did work under the guidance of Stryker, and, like Vachon, found it to be an enriching experience. Parks had grown up in the sort of rootless poverty that lies in the background of too many black Americans. The home in Kansas had broken up when his mother died and Gordon, aged fifteen, had begun to wander. A few years in Minnesota were followed by years in Seattle and later Chicago. Parks did odd jobs, worked as a waiter on a railroad, bartender, played semiprofessional basketball and football, and waited for something to happen. In 1939 he saw a magazine with pictures of the sinking of the *Panay* in China. The photographs excited him. About the same time he saw some FSA pictures and found them interesting. In Seattle he bought an old Voigtlander camera for $7.50 and began to take pictures.[18]

Back in the Minneapolis-St. Paul area, Parks began to take some interest in fashion photography. He handled several jobs successfully and was noticed by the wife of Joe Louis, who asked him to

Riding out to bring back
cattle, first stages of bliz-
zard, 1940. John Vachon.

come to Chicago to photograph a new line of ladies' fashions which she was preparing to market. Parks went along. He might have remained a fashion photographer; in fact part of his reputation as a photographer in later years would be based on his ability to take striking photographs of beautiful women. But Parks felt a need for something more; he wanted to be able to use his camera to speak of social problems.[19]

While he was working for Mrs. Louis in Chicago Parks met Jack Delano and became fascinated with the sort of work that he was doing. Delano, in turn, was impressed with the talent of the intense young man and encouraged him to develop his own directions. With the help of friends, Parks secured a grant from the Rosenwald Fund. The grant was more or less without stipulations and he was free of financial worries for a while. He chose to use the time working in Washington under Stryker's direction. With the help of Delano, Parks was brought into the organization in what might be described as an apprenticeship position. He was not paid, but Stryker enthusiastically took on the job of introducing him to the world of documentary photography.

> Roy, of course, put me through a very strict and revealing process in getting me acquainted with what was going on there, a very sharp, quick thing, (at times I thought rather brutal) but he had to shape me up rather quickly. He used a method of taking my camera away from me the first days I got there and sending me out in Washington to the theaters and department stores and drug stores and so forth — and I had some rather miserable experiences. . . . Suddenly they were saying, "We don't serve Negroes" ("Niggers" in some sections.) "You can't go to a picture show." Or, "No use stopping for we can't sell you a coat. . . ." And Roy more or less expected this, because he could see that I was green as a pea . . . and not too involved in humanity. . . . And I came back roaring mad and I wanted my camera and he said, "For what?" And I said I wanted to expose some of this corruption down here, this discrimination. So he says, "Well, you sit down here and write me a little paper on how you intend to do this." And I said, "Fine." So I wrote several papers and brought them in, but he kept after me until he got me down to one simple little project. That was my first lesson in how to approach a subject, that you didn't have to go in with all horns blasting away.[20]

Parks went through the rigorous initiation and emerged one of the best documentary photographers in the country. In later years he would work with Roy on other projects, in addition to doing extensive work for *Vogue* and *Life*.

The attack on Pearl Harbor on December 7, 1941, cut through the lives of Americans like a knife — suddenly everything was changed. Although the nation had been gearing for war for

Washington, D.C., 1942.
Gordon Parks.

months, the realization that the United States was actually in it
too, now, made everything different. For the historical section,
it meant that even more emphasis would be placed upon defense
pictures than had been in the past. After Pearl Harbor, it became
next to impossible to find time for the sort of loose, freewheeling
general assignments that the photographers had come to love.
Nobody had time to go South and "do cotton," or West and cover
the roundup in Montana. Instead the photographers were far more
likely to be found covering war industries, often from a point of
view that was decided far up the bureaucratic line, a point of
view that might or might not reflect their personal feelings.

The war affected the historical section in ways other than the
photographs they were asked to take. Bureaucratic changes came
that were sometimes beneficial, sometimes not. For a while, shortly after the beginning of the war, there was serious talk of moving
the entire Farm Security Administration to St. Louis.[21] Someone
far up the administrative ladder had the idea that the agency
would be more secure and closer to the agricultural heartland
there. From Stryker's point of view, such action would have been
a disaster. He was settled in very comfortable facilities; his political ties and administrative contacts were in Washington; nothing
but trouble could have come from such a change. The move did
not take place, but precious weeks were wasted while he and
other FSA administrators fought the proposal.

Far more serious was the fact that the agency was increasingly
being criticized as a major waster of federal funds. By 1941 and
early 1942, the enemies of the FSA were massing their forces
for a real attempt to have the entire agency done away with. Under
the influence of the American Farm Bureau Federation and the
Cotton Council, two organizations that represented the interests
of the large commercial farmers, Senators Harry F. Byrd of Virginia, Kenneth McKellar of Tennessee, Representative Everett
Dirksen of Illinois, and others began to probe for weaknesses
in the agency. Byrd succeeded in forming the Joint Committee
on Reduction of Nonessential Federal Expenditures and, as its
chairman, the Virginia conservative began an attack on the FSA.[22]

The congressional assault was carefully planned. In early 1942
the Farm Bureau Federation revealed that the FSA had paid the
poll taxes for many poor farmers in the South. By implication
the agency was charged with attempting to create a political ma-
chine. The spokesmen for the agency pointed out that its rural
loan programs were designed to clear up all outstanding debts for
farmers, and the poll tax was merely a part of the debt structure,

Truck driver at terminal, waiting to go out, Lynchburg, Virginia, 1943. John Vachon.

Broach used in finishing engine parts, Pratt and Whitney Aircraft Company, Hartford, Connecticut, 1941. John Collier. *Library of Congress*

but the enemies of the FSA pressed their case. From that point it was relatively easy to move on to a blanket indictment of the FSA for wasting the taxpayers' money on nonessential frills.[23] Naturally one of the frills was the photographic agency. As a tiny part of a very large organization, the historical section was never mentioned directly, but McKellar did condemn the organization for "paying clients' poll taxes, promoting socialized medicine, excessive spending on travel and *publicity* and wasting funds on no-account people [Italics added.]"[24] The implication was clear: if cuts were to be made, the historical section would be one of the first to suffer.

As the debate grew hotter, many people came to the aid of the FSA. Representative John H. Tolan of California led a nationwide investigation of the agency's migratory labor camps and concluded that they were a major positive force in the nation's war efforts.[25] Stryker and the photographers, very aware of the Tolan committee's work, supplied them with many photographs to illustrate their points.[26] Other major supporters included the gentlemanly Senator John Bankhead from Alabama and Milburn Wilson, respected dean of the extension service. But these men could at best fight only a holding action. The Byrd committee, urged on by E. A. O'Neal of the Farm Bureau Federation, was prepared to stop at nothing to weaken or ruin the FSA. Perhaps the low point in the debate came on May 18 when McKellar labeled C. B. Baldwin, FSA administrator, a Communist.[27] It was grandstanding of the worst sort and brought many conservatives to the defense of Baldwin, who was a Virginian by birth, and a gentle and loyal man. Richard Russell of Georgia noted that he had seldom agreed with "Beanie" Baldwin about anything, but he knew him well and felt, "He is as far from being a Communist as any man could possibly be."[28] Nevertheless the damage was done. When the debate was over, the budget of the Farm Security Administration had been cut 43 percent below the requested level for 1943, a cut that would leave the agency with a 27 percent smaller budget for the coming year.[29]

The budget cuts came in the early summer of 1942. They marked the beginning of the end, not only for the historical section, but for the entire FSA experiment at helping the lowest levels of rural people. All over the country, people who had resented the agency began to come out into the open. The Memphis *Commercial Appeal* published an editorial which was typical of the attitude of the established farming community. The hand of the Cotton Council was clear. "The F.S.A. has been vaccinated

New York City, 1942.
Arthur Rothstein.

with the Tugwellian virus and has fallen into the hands and under the blight of social gainers, do-gooders, bleeding hearts, and long-hairs who make a career of helping others for a price and according to their own peculiar, screwball ideas."[30] There had been criticism before, but in the overheated atmosphere of war it was becoming very serious indeed.

For Roy Stryker the changeover to a war-oriented government brought deep disappointments. He had seen the approaching situation as an opportunity to document the daily life processes of a nation at war with totalitarianism. Budget cuts and changes in the bureaucracy above him precluded this. For months after the budget fight of 1942, Stryker found himself embroiled in the bitterest bureaucratic infighting of his career. In order to maintain his office, he was forced to fall back on the tactics that had worked in earlier days: take in outside work for agencies that were established and popular in Congress, make the historical section necessary to them, and hope that they would speak up when the time came. By March, 1942, Stryker was doing work for the Office of War Information and writing to Russell Lee to justify the change. "As you know, the OWI is doing a very important job in the outside and inside of the country and their work is not going to be very much questioned by the brethren on the hill. In the meantime, we will be able to take on a lot of our regular Farm Security work."[31]

For a while the tactic worked. The photographers undertook a great deal of defense photography, but there also was time for the rural-oriented assignments too. It was a compromise, of course. The work for the OWI was often rather dull. The war agency required straight propaganda photographs; it had no use at all for the sort of thoughtful, probing, pictorial analysis that had become the hallmark of the historical section. Even so, the OWI duty meant working with pictures and it did keep things going. So long as one could return to the original projects, perhaps things would not be too bad.

In September, however, all the options were removed. The FSA was still under fire from those who wanted to economize and those who had never thought well of its programs. The historical section, with its long-range goals and rather nebulous approach, was hard to justify. Early that month a meeting took place in the office of C. B. "Beanie" Baldwin. Stryker remembered it this way: "I said, 'I think we ought to get out because you are in trouble. I think we ought to go to the OWI and get out of your hair.' And with tears in his eyes, he said to me, 'Roy, if you think you ought

Great Northern Railroad
grain elevators, Superior,
Wisconsin. John Vachon.

to stay and want to stay, I'll see you through some way.' I said, 'Beanie, you can't do it.' That was the time I left and he wept— he shed tears."[32]

And so the transition was made. Stryker and the historical section were no longer a part of the depression experiment to aid poor farmers. Like the President himself, they had been forced to make the change from "Dr. New Deal" to "Dr. Win-the-War." As an entity the historical section ceased to exist. It now became the photographic agency of the OWI. War propaganda became its full-time business.

Stryker was unhappy. Disputes arose over the status of his photographers. They had never had a civil service rating and now it began to hurt. He could not protect them from the draft nor could he get them supplies when they needed them. The team began breaking up. Arthur Rothstein returned to government service with the OWI when the war began, and for a while he and Roy worked together again. But in early 1943, it became clear that lack of civil service status made the draft a threat for all of the photographers. Rothstein joined the army and served the balance of the war in the Signal Corps as a part of an elite group of top photographers.[33] Russell Lee joined the air force and spent the war years making important aerial photographs of airfields in order to show pilots what to expect when they made their first approaches.[34] Bureaucratic interference from above trimmed most of the other photographers from Stryker's staff, and, by the spring of 1943, he found himself in a custodial position. He was expected to provide propaganda pictures from those already accumulated in the file, but little else.[35]

For Stryker the situation was intolerable. He would have to leave government service soon. Before he left, however, there was one important matter that had to be attended to. The photographic file, the principal legacy of eight years of hard work, had to be protected. The file had begun simply as a matter of course. It had seemed logical to keep the best of all pictures taken. In the early days, it had grown without any particular organization as photographers sent in their work. By the late 1930s John Vachon had succeeded in getting the file into usable shape. The pictures were kept in series as the photographers had shot them. For example, all of Rothstein's photographs of the Shenandoah Valley were kept together, as were all of Lee's pictures of Pie Town. The problem with this system came when one single type of picture was needed. If a newspaper or magazine wanted a shot of a girl standing in front of a log cabin, a clerk had to look through the file

Pittsburgh, Pennsylvania,
1941. John Vachon.

until he found what was needed. In 1942 a young expert in the field of archival organization, Paul Vanderbilt, was hired and reorganized the entire file in order to make photographs accessible by subject. By 1943 the work was well under way, and all 130,000 photographs were being filed and catalogued. The collection constituted a priceless heritage, yet it was in danger.[36]

The most virulent enemies of the FSA, both on Capitol Hill and within the federal bureaus, wanted the agency wiped out without a trace, and this meant that the photographic records would be destroyed. By September, 1943, however, Stryker was making plans to transfer the entire file to the Library of Congress. The plan was a good one. At the Library of Congress, the photographs would be entirely in the public domain and accessible to anyone who wanted to use them. The new head of the library was an old friend, Archibald MacLeish, whose love for the photographs was well established. "Archie" would see that nobody destroyed the file. The only thing necessary was to win approval for the planned transfer. Within the OWI, however, there existed serious opposition to such a plan. The New York office of the picture division of the OWI was run by a veteran Associated Press man named Tom Sears. The Associated Press had always disliked the work done by Stryker's government photographers and Sears was working to eliminate the file. There were others within the organization—who held personal grudges against Stryker from the earlier days of infighting—who would not help him, although they might not move actively against him either.

Writing unofficially, Stryker incisively assessed his position:

> I don't know how general our opposition is at the moment, but I do know we can expect trouble from two people. Tom Sears, who is in charge of the Picture Division in the New York office, is specifically in charge of handling visual materials. We feel certain that he would like to come down and pick out parts of the best materials in the file and move it up to New York. Furthermore, we feel certain that eventually, he will want to break up the whole outfit. . . . Tom is an old AP man and pretty thoroughly sold on the idea that Government should have nothing or do nothing that will interfere with the operations of the agencies. . . .
>
> George Lyon, who has just been made a Deputy of the OWI, has I am sure, taken a terrific dislike to me. I feel certain that George would go out of his way to smash this place.[37]

In order to get approval for his planned transfer of the file to the Library of Congress, Stryker simply avoided the OWI officials and went over their heads. In a letter to Jonathan Daniels, admin-

Punxsatawney, Pennsyl-
vania, 1940. Jack Delano.

istrative assistant to the President, Stryker pleaded his case directly to the top.

> The 130,000 photographs in this office contain the record of the
> war's impact on the domestic scene since 1942; the record of America
> from 1935 — the small town, the farm and the people — and the Admin-
> istration's record on the land during that time, the efforts of Resettle-
> ment, F.S.A., etc. This record is in one piece; the oldest pictures in
> it have been as valuable as the most recent to the Office of War Infor-
> mation in telling here and abroad the story of America at war. At
> present, this coverage, conceived and produced as an unbroken con-
> tinuity, is in danger of being dispersed.
> Preoccupation with the issues of the moment may now lead to the
> forcible separation of material dealing with today from the material
> of years before. Such dismemberment would be fatal, for this is a live,
> an active record. Out of America at peace grew the strength of America
> at war. This soil is the same soil and the people are the same people.
> It is possible to preserve the record intact and still make it available
> to the OWI and other war agencies for current use. This can be accom-
> plished by transferring the custody of the file to the Library of Congress
> with instructions to place it on loan to the OWI for the duration. This
> transfer would not mean additional expense to the Library, would pre-
> serve the whole record and would not hinder proper use by the Office
> of War Information.[38]

Daniels, who knew and respected the work of the historical
section, saw to the necessary details and the transfer was made.
Assured that his precious pictures were safe, Stryker resigned.

Stryker's letter of resignation to Elmer Davis, director of the
OWI, was short and to the point. Stryker pointed out that since
the transfer to the Office of War Information, the nature of his
job had changed. "The reduction of the number of photographers,
the decrease in the editorial staff, and the curtailment of distribution functions have changed the position from that of an editorial
director to that of an administrative operator."[39] Since Stryker
had always functioned as an editorial director, he felt that he
was no longer needed.

Stryker's resignation came as a shock to many of his old friends.
Florence Kellogg, of *Survey Graphic,* aging crusader and long-
time confidante, wrote to say how much she regretted that his
years with the government were coming to an end.[40] But the shock
of resignation hardly matched the surprise that greeted Stryker's
announcement that his next job would be as director of a major
project to document the work and the impact of Standard Oil of
New Jersey![41] Roy Stryker, liberal, son of a Populist, friend of the
poor, was going to work for Standard Oil! Even he seemed a little
surprised about the turn of affairs. He was tired of the struggle
for existence within a government bureaucracy. The directness

Roy Emerson Stryker.
Gordon Parks.

and simplicity of dealing within a large and wealthy corporation
was very attractive to him. Besides, the offer that Standard Oil
made was quite appealing from every standpoint.

The position with the corporation had been on the horizon for
several months before the break finally came. Ed Stanley, an old
friend of Roy's in Washington, had left government work and
had gone to Standard Oil. Stryker had seen him on occasional
visits to New York, and each time Stanley had talked about the
possibility of Roy's doing a major photographic project documenting the role and importance of oil, in terms of the men and ma-
chines that made the industry work.

Stryker was rather skeptical at first. "Ed," he said, "I have a
confession to make. When I was a boy, we were raised on the
concept of three great evils. My Populist father had a belief in
three evils which were Wall Street, the railroad, and Standard
Oil, and the greatest of these is Standard Oil!"[42] But Stanley persisted and eventually convinced his superior in the public relations
department that Stryker was just the man that Standard Oil needed
to upgrade its image. Earl Newsom, director of Standard's public
relations department, was a salesman's salesman. Once convinced
that Stryker was needed, he went to work. Stryker liked Newsom.
Years later, in an expansive mood, he recalled: "He was the slick-
est character I had ever seen. I don't know what he bathed in, but
he bathed every morning in some sort of emulsified oil, just to
make himself slick as possible!"[43]

Under Newsom's prodding Stryker submitted a list of detailed
needs for setting up a major photographic agency. There would
be four photographers at $100 a week, two secretaries at $35
and $45 a week, $10,000 a year for the director.[44] It all came to
a rather staggering sum. He sent off the list in August, 1943, and
sat back, expecting nothing to happen. It was a proposal, a starting
point. His idea was to set those management men back on their
heels a bit. Perhaps they thought that a photographic project could
be done cheaply; well, he would give them something to think
about! Two weeks later, to his total astonishment, word came
through that the management of Standard Oil had accepted his
proposal completely. In fact they felt that his estimates were too
low. Obviously, working for a large private corporation would
be quite a bit different from working within the framework of
a government bureaucracy. After eight years in the Washington
jungle, the new prospect looked very refreshing.

Stryker's attitude at the time of his leaving government service
shows clearly in a letter to his old friend Pare Lorentz.

After 5:30 tonight I will no longer be one of Uncle Sam's employees. I can't say that I am very happy about this separation, although I am not too sorry to be leaving the OWI. . . .

The Budget Boys and some of my "friends" in the Domestic Branch [OWI] surely did a nice job on this outfit. We awakened about July 12 with no photographers left. I know if I wanted to put up a Hell of a fight I could get them back again, but when the fight is over, we would look on an empty victory, I am sure. . . . The whole trend in Washington is too big for us to buck at this time. . . . The file project work goes on, and we have gotten the file itself safely tied up, I hope.

Monday morning I start to work for the Standard Oil Company of New Jersey. I know you are going to have a hemorrhage when you hear about it. But hold your hat until you get back and I tell you more about what happened. I presented them a memorandum. . . . The report was pretty tentative and all prices were pretty high, and I thought it would be a basis for discussion. To my surprise, they didn't see any need for discussing it, and their only comment was that they didn't think I had asked for enough.[45]

In October Roy Stryker left Washington permanently. His staff had already moved on to other things. His experiment was finished. Never again would the government engage in documentary photography on such a scale or with such skill. The photographs that his staff had taken had begun a new trend in American esthetics. They had taught that a picture could be beautiful and still possess a social conscience. The pictures had helped to galvanize public opinion behind programs to aid the rural poor (at least for a while), and they had recorded the texture and "feel" of life in the 1930s in a way that no other project has done.

For the most part, the people who worked under Stryker's direction continued careers in photography. Only Marion Post Wolcott chose to leave the active life of a traveling professional photographer, preferring the simpler and infinitely saner existence of a wife and mother.[46] Carl Mydans continued to work for *Life* after the war. He is still on the *Life* staff and continues active and influential work. Arthur Rothstein went back to *Look* when the war was over. He worked as a photographer and eventually became technical director, in charge of all visual aspects of the magazine until it ceased publication in 1971. His book *Photojournalism: Pictures for Magazines and Newspapers* is a standard work in its field. He continues to teach and lecture on photojournalism at Columbia University, where his patience and wit make him a popular teacher. Rothstein is also spending considerable time in government photography again. He has been asked by the Environmental Protection Agency to direct a major national documentary project on pollution. "Project Documerica," as it is called, will employ top photographers in an effort to create a visual record of the nation's development of a "new environmental ethic."[47]

Russell Lee worked with Stryker on the Standard Oil project for a while after the war. Since then he has successfully free-lanced for virtually every major magazine. Today he and his wife, Jean, live in Austin, Texas, where he teaches upper level courses in photographic esthetics. His students are encouraged to develop their own personal directions. Their work is highly individualistic, yet the influence of Stryker and the early documentary work is always there.[48] John Vachon's photographic career continued at *Look,* while *Life* utilized the work of Gordon Parks.

Among those whose influence has been greatest on American visual taste, the names Walker Evans and Dorothea Lange deserve a special place. Both have been featured in books and exhibits by the Museum of Modern Art in New York; both are among the first names mentioned when young photographers meet to discuss great styles and approaches. Although Evans' connection with the FSA project was relatively short and even stormy, much of his best work came during these years. His *American Photographs* stands today as one of the finest picture books ever done. Evans has worked on the staff of *Fortune* for many years and teaches classes in esthetics at Yale.[49] Dorothea Lange's death in 1965 robbed the world of visual art of one of its most sensitive citizens. A retrospective exhibition of her work was sponsored by the Museum of Modern Art in 1966. Her last major exhibition, *Dorothea Lange Looks at the American Country Woman,* was a visual poem to the strength and determination of farm women.[50] Both Lange and Evans contributed many of the best photographs included in two highly influential exhibits, *The Bitter Years* and *The Family of Man,* both done under the auspices of the Museum of Modern Art and under the direction of Edward Steichen.[51]

Of the later photographers who served in the FSA historical section, Jack Delano continued to work in the documentary field. He, like Lee, worked on the Standard Oil project for a time after the war. Today he directs the government's television service for the island of Puerto Rico. John Collier's career moved into the area of anthropology. He has pioneered in the field of using cameras to record the social and cultural aspects of anthropology that could not be noted in any other way. His recent book, *Visual Anthropology: Photography as a Research Method,* has already attained the status of a classic in its field.

The influence of the project director, Roy Stryker, who once

again is living in western Colorado, remains difficult to assess.
It is still growing. His work with Standard Oil continued for almost a decade, and later he carried out a major photo-documen-
tary project for Jones-Laughlin Steel Corporation. During these
years many of the nation's best photographers were discovered
and developed by Stryker. After retirement in the mid-fifties, he
continued to act as a consultant to major news magazines and
industrial house organs. His interest in young photographers
continued, involving him in many seminars and in teaching situations such as the University of Missouri's fine school of photojournalism. Many younger photographers who are working today
feel the force of his personality without even realizing it. Those
who have looked at hard-hitting photographic essays in the pages
of *Life* and *Look* and have learned from them have, in effect, felt
the guiding hand of Stryker. Carl Mydans has spoken for many
photographers when he said of Stryker: "No one ever worked for
him for any length of time without carrying some of Roy Stryker
with him. . . . In all the years since I left him, when making pictures I often hear him say, 'Now what are you doing that for?
Why are you making that picture?' I still feel I have to justify myself before him as I did when I worked for him."[52] Perhaps therein
lies his value. In order to be a great director of photographers,
Stryker had to first be a great teacher. With his breadth of experience and his deep love for the land, and with the immense force
of his personality, Stryker showed a nation its problems and its
greatness during the decade of the depression, and in so doing
permanently changed the direction of American photography.

Notes

INTRODUCTION

1 James L. McCamy, *Government Publicity, Its Practice in Federal Administration* (Chicago, 1939), 233.
2 *Ibid.,* 119. McCamy refers to Stryker's approach to government publicity as "a unique experimental plan."

CHAPTER I

1 Interview, Roy E. Stryker by F. J. Hurley, July 28, 29, 1967, Montrose, Colo. Memphis State University Office of Oral History Research. July 28, 1967. Transcribed, 18, hereinafter cited as Stryker-Hurley interview, with appropriate date.
2 John Durniak, "Focus on Stryker," *Popular Photography* (September, 1962), 61. Stryker was born in Great Bend, Kansas, in 1893. The family moved to Colorado when he was three.
3 Stryker-Hurley interview, July 28, 1967, p. 18.
4 *Ibid.,* 1.
5 Interview, Roy E. Stryker by Richard K. Doud, June 13, 1964, Montrose, Colo. Archives of American Art, Detroit. Transcribed, 2, hereinafter cited as Stryker-David interview, I, II.
6 Stryker-Hurley interview, July 28, 1967, p. 2.
7 Stryker-Doud interview, I, 3.
8 *Ibid.*
9 Stryker-Hurley interview, July 28, 1967, p. 4.
10 Stryker-Doud interview, I, 3.
11 Stryker-Hurley interview, July 28, 1967, p. 4.
12 *Ibid.,* 6.
13 Stryker-Doud interview, I, 5.
14 Stryker-Hurley interview, July 28, 1967, p. 5.
15 *Ibid.,* 6.
16 Stryker-Doud interview, I, 6.
17 Stryker-Hurley interview, July 28, 1967, p. 9.
18 *Ibid.*
19 *Ibid.,* 1, 6, 7.
20 Stryker-Doud interview, I, 6.
21 Roy Emerson Stryker, Personal File, Stryker Collection, University of Louisville Photographic Archive, hereinafter cited as Stryker, Personal File.
22 Stryker-Doud interview, I, 10.
23 *Ibid.,* 12.
24 Rexford G. Tugwell, Thomas Munro, and Roy E. Stryker, *American Economic Life* (New York, 1925), vii–x.
25 Perhaps the best sources of information on Mathew Brady are Robert Taft, *Photography and the American Scene: A Social History, 1839–1889* (New York, 1938); and James D. Horan, *Mathew Brady: Historian with a Camera* (New York, 1955).

26 See also Riis, *The Making of an American* (New York, 1901).
27 The best source of information on Lewis Hine is Judith Mara Gutman, *Lewis W. Hine and the American Social Conscience* (New York, 1968).
28 Beaumont Newhall, *The History of Photography from 1839 to the Present Day* (New York, 1949), 102. See also Waldo Frank, Lewis Mumford *et al.* (eds.), *America and Alfred Stieglitz: A Collective Portrait* (New York, 1934).
29 Stryker-Hurley interview, July 28, 1967, p. 13.
30 Tugwell *et al.* (eds.), *American Economic Life*, vii.
31 Stryker-Hurley interview, July 28, 1967, p. 13.
32 Stryker, Personal File.
33 Stryker-Doud interview, I, 11.
34 Interview, Arthur Rothstein by F. J. Hurley, August 14, 1968, New York. In possession of the author. Untranscribed, hereinafter cited as Rothstein-Hurley interview.
35 Stryker-Hurley interview, July 28, 1967, p. 7.

CHAPTER II

 1 Chester C. Davis, "The Development of Agricultural Policy Since the End of the World War," in United States Department of Agriculture, *Farmers in a Changing World: The Yearbook of Agriculture, 1940* (Washington, D.C., 1940), 298, 299.
 2 *Ibid.,* 304, 305.
 3 Ralph L. Dewey and James C. Nelson, "The Transportation Problem of Agriculture," *The Yearbook of Agriculture, 1940,* p. 725.
 4 Davis, "The Development of Agricultural Policy," 323–25. See also *First Annual Report of the Resettlement Administration* (Washington, D.C., 1936), 1.
 5 Paul V. Maris, "Farm Tenancy," *The Yearbook of Agriculture, 1940,* p. 889.
 6 Davis, "The Development of Agricultural Policy," 311.
 7 *Ibid.*
 8 Rexford G. Tugwell, *The Brains Trust* (New York, 1968), 21, 22. Also Bernard Sternsher, *Rexford Tugwell and the New Deal* (New Brunswick, N.J., 1964), 4. Tugwell grew up in a small town, but he knew and understood rural life. In one of his writings he stated: "To my children the life of my boyhood in that town Sinclairville, New York, would seem incredibly simple, no doubt. We went barefoot in summer; . . . made our own skis and sleds; and one of my daily duties was to go down to the pasture lot and bring up the cow for milking. . . . We had fourteen driving horses in the barn; I had a flock of chickens, a hutch of rabbits and a maple sugar house all my own." Rexford G. Tugwell, *The Stricken Land* (Garden City, 1947), 663.
 9 Sternsher, *Rexford Tugwell,* 4, 5.
10 Richard S. Kirkendall, *Social Scientists and Farm Politics in the Age of Roosevelt* (Columbia, Mo. 1966), 43. See also Sternsher, *Rexford Tugwell,* 5; and Tugwell, *The Brains Trust,* 407.
11 Sternsher, *Rexford Tugwell,* 11.
12 *Ibid.,* 6, 7.
13 *Ibid.,* 7.
14 Rothstein-Hurley interview.
15 Tugwell, *The Brains Trust,* 14, 15.
16 *Ibid.,* 19.
17 *Ibid.,* 5.
18 Kirkendall, *Social Scientists,* 42–44.

19 Sternsher, *Rexford Tugwell,* 46. Kirkendall, *Social Scientists,* 44, 45. Tugwell, *The Brains Trust,* 452–53.
20 Tugwell, *The Brains Trust,* 207. Sternsher, *Rexford Tugwell,* 88.
21 Sternsher, *Rexford Tugwell,* 88
22 Stryker-Hurley interview, July 28, 1967, pp. 1, 2. Phyllis Ann Stryker was born August 20, 1927.
23 *Ibid.,* 2.
24 *Ibid.,* 2, 3.
25 *Ibid.,* 3.
26 *Ibid.,* 4.
27 Rothstein-Hurley interview.
28 *Ibid.*
29 David E. Conrad, *The Forgotten Farmers: The Story of Sharecroppers in the New Deal* (Urbana, 1965), 27–36.
30 Arthur Raper, *Preface to Peasantry: A Tale of Two Black Belt Counties* (Chapel Hill, 1936), 34.
31 *First Annual Report of the Resettlement Administration,* 1.
32 *Ibid.,* 1, 2.
33 Eleanor Roosevelt, *This I Remember* (New York, 1949), 126–33.
34 Tugwell, *The Brains Trust,* 21–23.
35 Paul Conkin, *Tomorrow a New World: The New Deal Community Program* (Ithaca, 1959), 305–25.
36 Sidney Baldwin, *Poverty and Politics: The Rise and Decline of the Farm Security Administration* (Chapel Hill, 1968), 204–207.
37 *First Annual Report of the Resettlement Administration,* 1, 2.
38 Baldwin, *Poverty and Politics,* 221–25.
39 Stryker-Hurley interview, July 28, 1967, pp. 5, 6.
40 *Ibid.,* 17.

CHAPTER III

1 Stryker, Personal File.
2 *Ibid.*
3 *Ibid.*
4 Interview, Rexford Guy Tugwell and Grace Falke Tugwell by Richard K. Doud, January 21, 1965, Santa Barbara, Calif. Archives of American Art, Detroit. Transcribed, 7.
5 Stryker-Doud interview, I, 19.
6 *Ibid.*
7 *Ibid.*
8 *Ibid.*
9 Stryker to Harry F. Carman, October 11, 1935; Stryker to Carman, November 1, 1935; Stryker to Carman, December 7, 1935; Stryker Correspondence, Roy Stryker Collection, University of Louisville Photographic Archive, hereinafter cited as Stryker, Correspondence, Louisville.
10 Rothstein-Hurley interview.
11 *Ibid.*
12 J. G. Lootens, "The Story of Carl Mydans," *U.S. Camera* (December, 1939), 22, 23.
13 Stryker-Doud interview, I, 18.
14 *Ibid.,* 18.
15 Stryker in personal conversation with the author, July 28, 1967, Montrose, Colorado. For similar statement see Stryker-Doud interview, I, 20.
16 "Walker Evans," *The Encyclopedia of Photography* (20 vols.; New York, 1964), VII, 1,312.

17 *Ibid.,* 1,312. The French portraitist Paul Nadar was probably the best-known photographer in Europe in his day. His father had begun studio work in 1858 and had built a distinguished clientele when Paul took over in 1880. The Nadars were particularly well known for their use of artificial light. See "Nadar," *ibid.,* XIII, 2,484, 2,485.
18 *Ibid.,* 1,312.
19 Walker Evans, *American Photographs* (New York, 1938).
20 Interview, Lou Block by F. J. Hurley, December 19, 1967, Louisville, Kentucky. In possession of the author. Untranscribed.
21 Stryker-Doud interview, I, 21.
22 Walker Evans, Personal File, Stryker Collection.
23 Stryker in personal conversation with the author, July 28, 1967, Montrose, Colorado.
24 Seldon Rodman, *Portrait of the Artist as an American, Ben Shahn: A Biography with Pictures* (New York, 1949), 101–105.
25 Interview, Ben Shahn by Richard K. Doud, April 14, 1964, Roosevelt, New Jersey. Archives of American Art, Detroit. Transcribed, 16, hereinafter cited as Shahn-Doud interview.
26 Interview, Ben Shahn by Dr. Harlan Phillips, October 3, 1965, Roosevelt, New Jersey. Archives of American Art, Detroit. Transcribed, 38, 39.
27 Rodman, *Portrait of the Artist,* 116.
28 Shahn-Doud interview, 16.
29 Dorothea Lange, *Dorothea Lange: The Making of a Documentary Photographer,* Oral Interview conducted by Suzanne Riess, Berkeley, Calif., 1968 (Limited publication by Regional Oral History Office, Bancroft Library, Berkeley), 167.
30 *Ibid.,* 167.
31 Shahn-Doud interview, 16.
32 McCamy, *Government Publicity,* 119, 120.

CHAPTER IV

1 Baldwin, *Poverty and Politics,* 122, 187.
2 Interview, Dorothea Lange by Richard K. Doud, May 22, 1964, New York City. Archives of American Art, Detroit. Transcribed, 10, hereinafter cited as Lange-Doud interview.
3 Shahn-Doud interview, 12.
4 Interview, Carl Mydans by Richard K. Doud, April 19, 1964, Larchmont, New York. Archives of American Art, Detroit. Transcribed, 4. See also John Durniac, "Focus on Stryker," *Popular Photography* (September, 1962), 64. This same story was told in an annotated interview. Carl Mydans by F. J. Hurley, August 14, 1968, New York City. In possession of the author. Untranscribed.
5 J. Russell Smith, *North America* (New York, 1925), 209–12, 392.
6 Interview, Russell Lee by F. J. Hurley, December 24, 1967, Austin, Texas. Annotated. In possession of the author, hereinafter cited as Lee-Hurley interview.
7 R. E. Stryker to Walker Evans, undated [internal evidence indicates late spring, 1936]. Evans Correspondence, Stryker Collection.
8 *Ibid.*
9 *Ibid.*
10 Stryker to Evans, dated 1936 [internal evidence, including the fact that this letter was addressed to one of the last stops on Evans' projected itinerary, indicates that this letter postdates the letter cited just above]. Evans Correspondence.

11 Official Memo, M. E. Riordan to Evans, July 15, 1936, *ibid.*
12 James Agee and Walker Evans, *Let Us Now Praise Famous Men* (New York, 1941), xiv.
13 Lange-Doud interview, 21–22.
14 Dorothea Lange to R. E. Stryker, November 19, 1936, Lange Correspondence, Stryker Collection.
15 Lange to Stryker, September 30, 1936, *ibid.*
16 Stryker to Lange, October 30, 1935, *ibid.*
17 Stryker to Lange, January 14, 1936, *ibid.*
18 Lange to Stryker, February 24, 1936, *ibid.*
19 Lange to Stryker, December 31, 1935, *ibid.* Lange announced that she and Paul Taylor had recently been married. The two had been working together on migrant problems for about two years. It was a second marriage for both.
20 Lange to James Forty, May 29, 1936, *ibid.*
21 Lange-Doud interview.
22 Lange to Stryker, March 2, 1936, Lange Correspondence.
23 *Dorothea Lange* [Retrospective Exhibition, The Museum of Modern Art, New York, 1966], introductory essay by George P. Elliot, 7.
24 Stryker to Lange, September 18, 1935, Lange Correspondence.
25 Stryker to Lange, October 30, 1935, *ibid.*
26 Stryker to Lange, January 3, 1936, *ibid.*
27 Stryker-Doud interview, 5.
28 *Ibid.*
29 Letter of Authorization, Theodor Jung officially employed by R.A. as a "Photographic Illustrator," September 13, 1935. Official Pass to USDA Building, signed by John Franklin Carter, September 19, 1935. Unfiled miscellaneous collection, Prints and Photographs Division. Library of Congress. These letters were discovered by accident and are not a part of any formal group.
30 Stryker to Jung, April 13, 1936, *ibid.* Prints and Photographs Division, Library of Congress.
31 Memorandum, Adrian J. Dornbush, Director, Special Skills Division to A. A. Mercy, Chief, Information Division, June 30, 1936, acknowledge transfer of T. Jung from Information Division to Special Skills Division, *ibid.*
32 Lootens, "The Story of Carl Mydans," 23.
33 Russell Lee to Stryker, January 4, 1962, Lee Correspondence, Stryker Collection.
34 *Ibid.* See also Stryker to Lee, October 19, 1936, *ibid.*
35 Lee to Stryker, January 4, 1962, *ibid.*
36 Arthur Rothstein later recalled that the sewers in the Department of Agriculture Building used to back up into the developing sinks! Rothstein-Hurley interview.
37 *Ibid.* See also Rothstein to Stryker, October (no precise date), 1935, Rothstein Correspondence, Stryker Collection.
38 Rothstein-Hurley interview.
39 *Ibid.*
40 Arthur Rothstein, "The Picture That Became a Campaign Issue," *Popular Photography* (September, 1961), 42.
41 *Ibid.*, 43. See also Rothstein to Stryker, April 6, 18, 23, 1936; Stryker to Rothstein, June 9, 1936. Rothstein Correspondence, Stryker Collection.
42 Rothstein, "The Picture That Became a Campaign Issue," 43.
43 Fargo *Forum*, August 27, 1936.

44 *Ibid.*

45 New York *Herald Tribune,* August 29, 1936; New York *Sun,* August 29, 1936; Billings (Mont.), *Gazette,* September 1, 1936; Akron, Ohio, *Beacon,* September 8, 1936; Toledo (Ill.), *Democrat,* September 24, 1936; Greenfield (Ill.), *Argus,* September 25, 1936; Oskaloosa, Iowa, *Herald,* September 15, 1936. These examples could be multiplied many times.

46 Erie (Pa.), *Dispatch-Herald,* September 7, 1936.

47 Edwin Locke was appointed assistant chief of the historical section, April 16, 1936. See memo, Edwin Locke to George Barnes, no date, Stryker Correspondence. Archives of American Art, Detroit. Locke remained in this position until the autumn of 1937 when he left to work on the staff of a New York magazine. In the spring of 1938 he returned to the historical section. Within a year he had left again to work with the United States Film Service under Pare Lorentz. Stryker remembered Locke as an extremely able, but unstable young man. Stryker to Locke, April 25, 1938, Stryker Correspondence. Archives of American Art, Detroit, hereinafter cited as Stryker Correspondence, Detroit. Stryker in personal conversation with the author, July 28, 1967, Montrose, Colorado.

48 Undated press release, Stryker Collection.

49 Edwin Locke to Arthur Rothstein, August 29, 1936, Rothstein Correspondence, Stryker Collection.

50 New York *Herald Tribune,* September 6, 1936.

51 Rothstein, "The Picture That Became a Campaign Issue," 43.

52 *U.S. Camera Annual,* 1937.

53 M. E. Gilfond appears to have become Chief of the Information Division during the summer of 1936. The first letter to mention him is Stryker to Lange, October 7, 1936, Lange Correspondence.

54 *Ibid.* Stryker actually wrote, "I am now down to two photographers, Rothstein and Mydans." Since Mydans had already gone to *Life* and Lee had already joined the staff, I have assumed that Stryker or his secretary simply wrote the wrong name.

55 Stryker to Lange, October 22, 1936, *ibid.*

56 Stryker to Lange, January 22, 1937, *ibid.*

CHAPTER V

1 "Our going to Agriculture has given us a new lease on life, we hope. There are so many things that we can do pictorially, not only for Resettlement, but for Agriculture." R. E. Stryker to Dorothea Lange, December 21, 1936, Letters in Photography, Dorothea Lange, Stryker Collection. For information on the transfer, the Bankhead-Jones Farm Tenancy Act, and effects on the agency in general, see Baldwin, *Poverty and Politics,* 187–88.

2 *Ibid.,* 190–91.

3 *Ibid.,* 121. See also, Wilma Dykeman and James Stokley, *Seeds of Southern Change: The Life of Will Alexander* (Chicago, 1962), 122.

4 Dykeman and Stokely, *Seeds of Southern Change,* 227.

5 Baldwin, *Poverty and Politics,* 111.

6 Robert Lynd and Helen M. Lynd, *Middletown: A Study In American Culture* (New York, 1929).

7 Stryker, Personal File. The entire shooting script is reprinted in Thomas H. Garver (ed.), *Just Before the War: Urban America from 1935 to 1941 as Seen by Photographers of the Farm Security Administration* (Boston, 1968), 9.

8   There is some confusion as to the origin of the small-town study. The actual shooting script cites the conversation with Lynd. In one interview, however, Stryker remembered the idea as coming from Ruth Goodhue, an editor of *Architectural Forum.* Stryker-Doud interview, II, 36.

9   Garver, *Just Before the War,* 9, 10.

10 *Ibid.,* 10.

11 Sherwood Anderson, *Home Town: The Face of America* (New York, 1940).

12 Werner J. Severin, "Photographic Documentation by the Farm Security Administration, 1935–1941" (M.A. thesis, University of Missouri, 1959), 22, 23.

13 Richard Wright and Edwin Rosskam, *Twelve Million Black Voices: A Folk History of the Negro in the United States* (New York, 1941).

14 Locke to Stryker, February 4, 1937, Stryker Correspondence, Detroit.

15 Stryker to Locke, February 13, 1937, *ibid.*

16 Lee-Hurley interview.

17 *Ibid.*

18 *Ibid.*

19 Garver, *Just Before the War,* 9.

20 Lee-Hurley interview.

21 William E. Leuchtenburg, *Franklin D. Roosevelt and the New Deal* (New York, 1963), 245.

22 A personality clash developed between Stryker and Evans rather early in the project. There was some disagreement over pictures (which were good and which were not) and subject matter. More serious was Evans' insistence upon being left completely alone while photographing, his unwillingness to receive direction, and his relatively low output. When word came that the budget would be cut in late 1937, Evans was, from Stryker's point of view, the logical person to leave. Stryker-Hurley interview, July 27, 1967. Notes in possession of author.

23 Stryker to Lange, October 16, 1937, Lange Correspondence.

24 Rothstein to Stryker, May 26, 1938; Stryker to Rothstein, May 27, 1938; Rothstein to Stryker, June 24, 1938, Rothstein Correspondence.

25 Stryker to Lee, September 2, 1938, Lee Correspondence.

26 Lee to Clara Dean Wakeham, (Stryker's secretary), September 12, 1938, *ibid.*

27 Lee-Hurley interview.

28 Lee to Stryker, September 16, 1938, Lee Correspondence.

29 Leuchtenburg, *Franklin D. Roosevelt,* 257.

30 Interview, Marion Post Wolcott by Richard K. Doud, January 18, 1965, Mill Valley, California, 1, 2. Archives of American Art, Detroit.

31 *Ibid.,* 3.

32 Severin, "Photographic Documentation," 21.

33 Rothstein to Stryker, January 27, 1939, Rothstein Correspondence.

34 Lange to Stryker, February 16, 1937, Lee Correspondence.

35 Rothstein to Stryker, January 16, 1939, Rothstein Correspondence.

36 Dykeman and Stokely, *Seeds of Southern Change,* 240, 241.

37 Rothstein to Stryker, March 7, 1937, Rothstein Correspondence.

38 Lee to Stryker, April 19, 1939, Lee Correspondence. See also Mark Adams and Russell Lee, "Our Town in East Texas," *Travel,* XL (March, 1940), 5–12.

39 Stryker to Lee, April 20, 1940, Lee Correspondence. See also Russell Lee, "Pie Town, New Mexico," *U.S. Camera* (October, 1941), 41.

40 John Collier, Jr., *Visual Anthropology: Photography as a Research Method* (New York, 1967).

CHAPTER VI

1 Lillian Perrine Davis, "Relief and the Sharecropper," *Survey Graphic,* (January, 1936), 20, 22.
2 Paul S. Taylor, "Again the Covered Wagon," *ibid.* (July, 1935), 348–51. 368. (six illustrations by Dorothea Lange.) Also Lucretia Penny, "Pea-Picker's Child," *ibid.,* 352, 353. (two illustrations by Dorothea Lange.)
3 Photograph by Lewis Hine, "Yielding Place to New," frontispiece, *ibid.* (January, 1934), Arthur E. Morgan, "Benchmarks in the Tennessee Valley" (three illustrations by Lewis Hine for TVA), *ibid.,* 5–10.
4 Rothstein-Hurley interview.
5 Stryker to Lange, March 23, 1937, Lange Correspondence.
6 "Children of the Forgotten Man," *Look,* March, 1937, 18–19 (*Look* was a monthly at this point); "Caravans of Hunger," *Look,* May 25, 1937, 18–19. (*Look* was published on a bi-monthly basis by May, 1937.) "Life on the Farm," *Look,* October 12, 1937, 16–21.
7 Edwin W. Embree, "Southern Farm Tenancy: A Way Out of Its Evils," *Survey Graphic,* (March, 1936), 149–53.
8 Dorothea Lange, "Draggin'-Around People," *ibid.,* (March, 1936), 524–25.
9 Paul Schuster Taylor, "From the Ground Up," *ibid.* (September, 1936), 526–29, 537–38.
10 *First Annual Report of the Resettlement Administration* (Washington, D.C., 1936).
11 *U.S. Camera 1937* (New York, 1937), 51, 52, 187, 193.
12 Stryker to Dorothea Lange, October 22, 1936, Lange Correspondence. See also catalogue, *Documentary Photographs: From the Files of the Resettlement Administration,* A College Art Association Exhibition, 1935, Stryker File, Stryker Collection.
13 Lange to Locke, September 10, 1936, Lange Correspondence.
14 Lee to Stryker, January 9, 1937, Lee Correspondence.
15 Louis W. Sipley, "Willard Morgan" (obituary), *Infinity* (November, 1967), 19.
16 Rothstein-Hurley interview.
17 Stryker to Locke, April 26, 1938, Stryker Correspondence, Detroit.
18 *Ibid.*
19 Elizabeth McCausland, "Rural Life in America as the Camera Shows It," Springfield *Sunday Union and Republican* (Springfield, Mass., September 11, 1938).
20 *Ibid.*
21 *Ibid.* See also Walker Evans, *American Photographs* (New York, 1938).
22 Stryker to Locke, April 26, 1938, Stryker Correspondence, Detroit.
23 Quotes for 1938 Grand Central Exhibition, Stryker Personal File.
24 *U.S. Camera 1938* (New York, 1938), 43–75.
25 Stryker to Lange, December 22, 1938, Lange Correspondence.
26 Rupert B. Vance, *How the Other Half is Housed: A Pictorial Record of Sub-Minimum Farm Housing in the South* (Chapel Hill, 1936).
27 Erskine Caldwell and Margaret Bourke-White, *You Have Seen Their Faces* (New York, 1937).
28 C. A. Pierce to Roy Stryker, June 7, 1937, Stryker Personal File.
29 Joseph Henry Jackson, "A Bookman's Notebook" (review of Archibald MacLeish's *Land of the Free*) San Francisco *Chronicle,* March 8, 1938.
30 From Archibald MacLeish, *Land of the Free* (New York, 1938), 84–88. And see Pare Lorentz, "We Don't Know" (review of *Land of the Free*), *Saturday Review,* April 2, 1938.
31 H. C. Nixon, *Forty Acres and Steel Mules* (Chapel Hill, 1938).

32   Interview, C. B. Baldwin by F. J. Hurley, August 18, 1967, Greenwich, Connecticut. Memphis State University Office of Oral History Research. Transcribed, 26, 27.

33   Dorothea Lange and Paul Schuster Taylor, *American Exodus: A Record of Human Erosion* (1939; rev. ed., New Haven, 1969).

34   *Ibid.*, 153, 154.

35   Lange to Stryker, December 7, 1938; Stryker to Lange, December 22, 1938; Lange to Stryker, May 16, 1939, Lange Correspondence.

36   Stryker to Rothstein, June 22, 1939, Rothstein Correspondence.

37   Stryker to Lange, October 31, 1939, Lange Correspondence.

38   Arthur F. Raper and Ira DeA. Reid, *Sharecroppers All* (Chapel Hill, 1941).

39   Adams and Lee, "Our Town in East Texas"; Lee, "Pie Town, New Mexico."

40   Charles R. Walker, "Homesteads—New Style," *Survey Graphic* (June, 1939), 377–81, 408 (five photographic illustrations by FSA). Lewis T. Nordyke, "Mapping Jobs for Texas Migrants," *ibid.* (March, 1940), 152–57 (five photographic illustrations by FSA).

41   Stryker to Dorothy Fontain (New York Committee to Aid Agricultural Workers), May 23, 1940. Fontain to Stryker, June 6, 1940. Stryker to Fontain, June 11, 1940, Farm Security Administration File, National Archives, Washington, D.C. Elodie Courter, Director, Department of Circulating Exhibitions, Museum of Modern Art, New York to Stryker, June 25, 1940, Farm Security Administration File, National Archives, Washington, D.C.

42   Garford L. Wilkinson, Regional Information Advisor, FSA Region 12 to John Fischer, Director of Information, FSA, January 18, 1940, Farm Security Administration File.

43   Lange to Stryker, March 12, 1939; Stryker to Lange, March 4, 1939, Lange Correspondence.

44   Hartley E. Howe, "You Have Seen Their Pictures," *Survey Graphic*, (April, 1940), 236–38.

45   *Ibid.*, 238.

46   Edward Stanley, "Roy Stryker—Photographic Historian," *Popular Photography* (July, 1941), 28–29, 100.

CHAPTER VII

1   Interview II, Arthur Rothstein by F. J. Hurley, August 16, 1968, at Rothstein's home, New Rochelle, New York. In possession of the author. Untranscribed. Stryker to Vernon Pope (managing editor, *Look*) April 6, 1940, Stryker Correspondence, Louisville. Stryker wrote to Pope: "I hate like Hell to lose the boy, but you take him with my blessing. It is going to be an excellent experience for him, and I am certain that he is going to serve you people very well."

2   Stryker to Jack Delano, March 28, 1940, Delano Correspondence, Stryker Collection.

3   Stryker-Doud interview, II, 7.

4   Stryker to Delano, September 12, 1940, Stryker Collection.

5   Delano to Stryker, January 14, 1941, *ibid.*

6   Delano to Wakeham (Stryker's secretary), October 24, 1940, *ibid.*

7   Arthur F. Raper, with FSA photographs by Jack Delano, *Tenants of the Almighty* (New York, 1943). See also news article "Delano Photographs Green County," Greenboro (Ga.) *Herald-Journal,* in Delano Correspondence, Stryker Collection.

8 Stryker to Delano, May 6, 1941, Delano Correspondence, Stryker Collection.

9 Taped memoirs made by John Collier for Roy Stryker, March, 1959. Detroit Archives of American Art.

10 Collier to Stryker, undated. September, 1941. Stryker, Personal File.

11 Collier to Stryker, undated, probably late September or early October, 1941, *ibid.*

12 Collier to Stryker, undated, "Tuesday Night," early September, 1941, *ibid.*

13 Collier to Stryker, undated, mid-September, 1941, *ibid.*

14 Collier to Stryker, probably early October, 1941, *ibid.*

15 Interview, John Vachon by Richard K. Doud, April 28, 1964, New York. Archives of American Art, Detroit. Transcribed, 1, 2.

16 *Ibid.,* 7–8.

17 *Ibid.,* 8–9.

18 Interview, Gordon Parks by Richard K. Doud, April 28, 1964, New York. Archives of American Art, Detroit. Transcribed, 1–2.

19 *Ibid.,* 4–5.

20 *Ibid.,* 6–7.

21 Stryker to Delano, December 22, 1941, Delano Correspondence, Stryker Collection.

22 Baldwin, *Poverty and Politics,* 347.

23 *Ibid.,* 350.

24 *Ibid.,* 356. Baldwin cites *Senate Hearings,* Agricultural Appropriations (1943), 77th Cong., 2nd. Sess., 686–706, 716–26, 734–853.

25 *Ibid.,* 354–55.

26 Stryker to Russell Lee, May 23, 1941, Lee Correspondence.

27 Baldwin, *Poverty and Politics,* 358. Baldwin cites *Congressional Record,* vol. 88, p. 4,286.

28 *Ibid.*

29 *Ibid.,* 359–61.

30 Editorial, Memphis (Tenn.) *Commercial Appeal,* May 25, 1943, quoted in Baldwin, *Poverty and Politics,* 284.

31 Stryker to Lee, March 18, 1942, Lee Correspondence.

32 Stryker-Hurley interview, July 28, 1967.

33 Rothstein-Hurley interview, II.

34 Lee to Stryker, January 4, 1962. Typed memoir in possession of University of Louisville Photographic Archive.

35 Stryker to Pare Lorentz, October 2, 1943, Stryker, Personal File.

36 Memorandum, Paul Vanderbilt to Archibald MacLeish, chief librarian, Library of Congress, June, 1943, Stryker, Personal File. The reorganization of the photographic file came, in this author's opinion, at a bad time. The file was passing from current use to historical use. The system that Vachon had followed was better suited to the needs of the social historian. Today, if one wishes to see what life was like in San Augustine, Texas, for example, the entire file must be searched for Lee's pictures, which are scattered throughout under arbitrary subject headings. Vanderbilt's system would have been better suited to the project during its active phase.

37 Private memorandum, Stryker to Jonathan Daniels, administrative assistant to the President, September 13, 1943, Stryker, Personal File.

38 Stryker to Daniels, September 13, 1943 (official letter), Stryker, Personal File.

39 Official Resignation, Roy E. Stryker, September 14, 1943. Stryker, Personal File.

40 Florence Kellogg to Stryker, September 24, 1943, Stryker, Personal File.

41 Stryker to Kellogg, September 28, 1943, *ibid.*
42 Stryker-Hurley interview, July 29, p. 22.
43 *Ibid.*
44 Memorandum to Earl Newsom from Stryker, August, 1943, Stryker, Personal File. The total estimate came to $1,553.30 per week!
45 Stryker to Lorentz. October 2, 1943, Stryker, Personal File.
46 Wolcott-Doud interview.
47 Arthur Rothstein, *Photojournalism: Pictures for Magazines and Newspapers* (Philadelphia, 1965). Rothstein-Hurley interview, II. Washington *Post*, May 14, 1972, E5.
48 Lee-Hurley interview. Also, "Autobiography," in *Russell Lee: Retrospective Exhibition, 1934–1964* (Austin, 1965).
49 "Walker Evans," *The Encyclopedia of Photography*, VII, 1,310–1,312.
50 Dorothea Lange, *Dorothea Lange Looks at the American Country Woman* (1967, Fort Worth). Lange, *Dorothea Lange* (New York, 1966).
51 Edward Steichen (ed.), *The Family of Man* (New York, 1955). Edward Steichen (ed.), *The Bitter Years, 1935–1941: Rural America as Seen by the Photographers of the Farm Security Administration* (New York, 1962). An even more recent exhibition, and one of the best, is Garver (ed.), *Just Before the War* (Boston, 1968).
52, Quoted in Durniak, "Focus on Stryker," 80.

Bibliography

PRIMARY SOURCES

Collections

Stryker, Roy, Collection, University of Louisville Photographic Archive. (This collection is the most complete source of letters and clippings pertaining to the Farm Security Administration historical section available.)

Stryker, Roy, Correspondence, Archives of American Art, Detroit. (The Archives of American Art has a fine series of interviews by Richard K. Doud which were extremely useful. Their collection of letters and papers is also extensive.)

Farm Security Administration File, Social and Economic Records Division and National Archives Records Service, Washington, D.C.

Farm Security Administration Collection, Prints and Photographs Division, Library of Congress. (This collection contains by far the most complete set of FSA photographs available. Eighty thousand of the original prints are maintained and are available to the public at a nominal cost.)

Unfiled Miscellaneous Letters, Prints and Photographs Division, Library of Congress. (This is not a formal collection, but is merely a small group of letters from Stryker to Theodor Jung that have been kept in the Prints and Photographs Division. They were uncovered briefly, microfilmed by the author, and returned to their brown paper bag on the back of a large filing cabinet.)

Interviews

Baldwin, C. B., interview by F. J. Hurley, August 18, 1967, Greenwich, Connecticut. Memphis State University Office of Oral History Research. Transcribed.

Block, Lou, interview by F. J. Hurley, December 19, 1967, Louisville, Kentucky. In possession of the author. Untranscribed.

Lange, Dorothea, interview by Richard K. Doud, May 22, 1964, New York City. Archives of American Art, Detroit. Transcribed.

Lange, Dorothea, *Dorothea Lange: The Making of a Documentary Photographer.* Oral Interview by Suzanne Ries, Berkeley, California, 1968. Limited publication by Regional Oral History Office, Bancroft Library, Berkeley.

Lee, Russell, interviewed by F. J. Hurley, December 24, 1967, Austin, Texas. Annotated. In possession of the author.

Mydans, Carl, interview by Richard K. Doud, April 19, 1964, Larchmont, New York. Archives of American Art, Detroit. Transcribed.

Mydans, Carl, interview by F. J. Hurley, August 14, 1968, New York City. In possession of the author. Untranscribed.

Parks, Gordon, interview by Richard K. Doud, April 28, 1964, New York, Archives of American Art, Detroit. Transcribed.

Rothstein, Arthur, interview by F. J. Hurley, August 14, 16, 1968, New York City. In possession of the author. Untranscribed.

Shahn, Ben, interview by Richard K. Doud, April 14, 1964, Roosevelt, New Jersey. Archives of American Art, Detroit. Transcribed.

Shahn, Ben, interview by Dr. Harlan K. Phillips, October 3, 1965, Roosevelt, New Jersey. Archives of American Art, Detroit. Transcribed.

Stryker, Roy E., interview by Richard K. Doud, June 13, 1964, Montrose, Colorado. Archives of American Art, Detroit. Transcribed.

Stryker, Roy E., interview by F. J. Hurley, July 28 and 29, 1967, Montrose, Colorado. Memphis State University Office of Oral History Research. Transcribed.

Tugwell, Rexford Guy and Grace Falke Tugwell, interview by Richard K. Doud, January 21, 1965, Santa Barbara, California. Archives of American Art, Detroit. Transcribed.

Vachon, John, interview by Richard K. Doud, April 28, 1964, New York. Archives of American Art, Detroit. Transcribed.

Wolcott, Marion Post, interview by Richard K. Doud, January 18, 1965, Mill Valley, California. Archives of American Art, Detroit. Transcribed.

Theses and Papers

Frankel, Ronni Ann, "Photography and the Farm Security Administration: The Visual Politics of Dorothea Lange and Ben Shahn." Senior Honors Thesis, Cornell University, 1969.

Hurley, F. J., "Photographing and Publicizing Farm Problems in the Southwest During the Depression: Documentary Photography and the Farm Security Administration." Paper read before the Texas State Historical Association, Spring, 1970.

Severin, Werner J., "Photographic Documentation by the Farm Security Administration, 1935–1941." M.A. thesis, University of Missouri, 1959.

PAMPHLETS USING FSA PHOTOGRAPHS

America's Land. Washington, D.C., 1936.

Farm Tenancy—The Remedy: Twenty Questions Asked and Answered. Washington, D.C., nd., probably 1937).

Resettlement Administration. Washington, D.C., 1936.

EARLY MAGAZINE ARTICLES—PHOTOGRAPHIC ESSAYS AND MISCELLANEOUS

"Best Pictures of 1937," *U.S. Camera, 1937.* New York, 1937. This was an annual, although it was not designated as such in the title. Individual FSA pictures may be found on pp. 51, 52, 139, 187, and 193.

"Caravans of Hunger," *Look,* May 25, 1937, 18–19. Look had only recently become a bimonthly publication.

"Children of the Forgotten Man," *Look,* March, 1937, 18–19. At this point, *Look* was still being published monthly.

"Life on the Farm," *Look,* October 12, 1937, 16–21.

"Pictures from the F.S.A.," *U.S. Camera Annual, 1938.* New York, 1938. pp. 43–75.

OTHER MAGAZINE ARTICLES USING FSA PHOTOGRAPHS

Adams, Mark and Russell Lee. "Our Town in East Texas," *Travel* (March, 1940), 5–12.

Davis, Lillian Perrine. "Relief and the Sharecropper," *Survey Graphic* (January, 1936), 20–22.

Embree, Edwin W. "Southern Farm Tenancy: A Way Out of Its Evils," *Survey Graphic* (March, 1936), 149–53.